Outside

Sales

Badass

Sell It Like You Got a Pair

XXX XXX XXX

WRITTEN BY,

RICHARD RAMSEY

DEDICATION

I WOULD LIKE tO DEDICAtE tHIS BOOK tO tHOSE MEn/WOMEn tHAt HAVE GIVEn tHEIR LIVES tO ANY CAUSE...

I tHAnK tHE FOLLOWING PEOPLE:

- MY WIFE tO BE
- MY FRIENDS/FAMILY
- MY SON
- MY MOM, DAD, BROtHER, AND SISTER

I tHAnK tHE CREAtORS OF tHESE PRODUCtS:

- ROCKStAR ENERGY DRINKS
- UNCRUStABLES
- CHULULA

CHAPTER LINEUP

INTRODUCTION

This is where I obviously introduce you to the book and the basic premise of it.

CHAPTER 1

Do you really have the brass for this job?

Tough job, not everyone can hack it... can you?

CHAPTER 2

Selling 'vs' transacting

Are you actually selling it or simply assisting the customer in buying it?

CHAPTER 3

It is about time you grew a pair!

Confidence! That's what this game is all about. How to grow a set!

CHAPTER 4

Stereotypists type to a beat

Fighting the stereotypes to become the salesperson THEY want.

CHAPTER 5

Pounding the pavement
If you can't get in front of people, you aren't going to make many sales.

CHAPTER 6

Asking questions and closing the sale
Talking to the customer, handling objections, and closing out the sale.

CHAPTER 7

Not your average crap bag
Dealing with competition and using it to your advantage.

CHAPTER 8

Milking the cow
Working your customer base to create a steady referral flow and long term success.

CHAPTER 9

Become the Badass
Putting everything together to finally become the badass you were born to be.

INTRODUCTION

I would hope that by simply reading the title of the book you have already come to the conclusion that I am not Tony Robbins. I am sure that you have also realized that this isn't going to be your typical book on selling. The whole purpose of the book was to create something that is realistic to what you actually see in outside sales. When I first started in sales, I looked everywhere for guidance and never really found anything that worked specifically for me. Over time, I created my own methods for selling that not only seemed to work for me, but worked well for many others as well. It was for this reason that I decided that I needed to create a book that actually focused on what is experienced in the real world.

I have read numerous books on sales throughout the years and for some reason they all sound alike. I would like to think this is because there is only one approach to selling, but there really isn't. The problem is that every jack bag with a computer thinks that they can write a book these days. While this may be the case, far too often than not, the writer has little to no actual experience in the field. Those that do have experience in the field are better at talking about how to do things than the actual application of their knowledge. So what I have found is that book after book I am given the same fluffed up crap information that only works in the most ideal of situations. The other problem is that many of the books are written as if you are selling a car. I sold cars at one time and I was damn good at it, but I can honestly say that there is virtually no connection between the two. This is why I have seen so many car salespeople come to outside sales and fail miserably. Hopefully, this book will assist those in outside sales at selling products/services in a manner that you just can't get from a traditional sales book.

There are a few things that you should keep in mind while reading this book.

1. I am by no means a writer. If you judge me based on my literary talents, you are missing the point. This book wasn't meant to be an English primer, it was meant to teach you how to make some green. If you don't want to make more money, then stop reading now. If I misspell a word, lets assume that I was such a rebel that I told my spellchecker it was wrong. If I use a bad sentence, have a run-on, then lets assume that I did it because I am real person. I don't have a degree in sales, I have a background in it. I have knowledge from

the streets and that is far more important than anything that you could ever learn in a book (funny… since this is a book). Bottom line: judge the material not the crap show that is my writing.

2. I'm not writing this book to be the most professional. I don't apologize for my random swearing, that's who I am. If you learn nothing else from me, personality is king in sales. If you can't stand out from the crowd, then your competition will walk on you. This doesn't mean that you should tell racial jokes while you are with your customers it means that you need to have a personality. If you can't pick up my personality throughout this book, then I didn't do my job. If you confuse me with another writer, then I DEFINITELY didn't do my job. Sometimes it takes a better person to outsell a better salesperson. So again, I may not be the most professional or politically correct but I am real. My customers know that I am real and it is a lot easier to be confident as yourself than it is to be confident as a sales robot.

3. Tony Robbins, Zig Ziglar, and those other so called sales professionals are incredible at sales THEORY. That shit doesn't work for

me, but it may very well work for someone else. Sometimes it is EASIER to be one of the sheep, than it is to be the bull, so if you follow those methods, good on you, way to be a sheep. If you want to be THE BULL, maybe you should stop following what everyone else is doing and learn a new method. If nothing else, it may very well help you to sell the customer that seems to have a response for everything you toss at them.

4. I am going to walk all over virtually every tenet of selling. Why? Because they simply didn't work for me. Closing techniques? Are you kidding me?   Everyone knows those, including the customers, so it is important to close the deal without letting the customer know that you are closing the deal. You may be in this purely for the commission, but it is important that you give the impression that you actually give a damn about helping the customer get the correct product/service to fit their needs.

5. More than anything, you are going to learn to be a creative salesperson. You are going to learn to generate leads and how to sell those customers once you have them. Anyone can close an inbound lead, but if

you can't close a creative lead you are never going to make the big money. So a lot of my focus is going to be on generating more leads so that there is more opportunity to sell. A horrible salesperson can outsell a great one by simply having a greater number of leads. The sooner you realize this, the sooner you will learn to succeed.

I think we have established that I am not going to wow you with the same traditional 'crap in the box' method of selling. I do however think it is important that you have a better understanding of what I really want to accomplish with this book. I wrote this book as a means of teaching those that aren't traditional salespeople.

My father wasn't a salesperson, nor was my mother. I never went to one of the elite business schools. I have a degree, but that has nothing to do with my true selling ability. Everything that I currently know about selling is by NOT selling. What I found was that while there were numerous books, audio tapes, and the like about selling, everyone was basically saying the same thing. The problem is that most of these closing techniques I had heard prior to ever getting in to sales. To me this meant that, if I knew it, so would the people that I would talk to. That's like playing a game of football against a team that has your playbook. You wouldn't do it in sports, so why the hell would you do it in something as competitive as sales? This puts you at a huge disadvantage before you ever even open your mouth. However, it took numerous failures for me to truly understand this. I quickly began to play around with a variety of styles and learned that when I was myself, I sold far more than I would by using pushy sales techniques. I also realized that I could sell the product for more, because I now had the confidence of the customer. This of course meant that they were much more willing to tell their friends/family about me.

While it doesn't make a whole lot of sense now, throughout the book you are going to learn how I went from always closing, to always assisting. Customers are smarter than they ever were in the past. They know our tricks and are waiting for our closing techniques. However, if you throw them off guard and change up the game, they don't have the ability to react, because they didn't rehearse it. Through the book I hope to teach you how to do this in a manner that will fit with any personality type and should be easily implemented regardless of what industry you work for.

The major thing that you have to remember is that you are ultimately the one in charge of your destiny. If you don't apply the concepts that I talk about, then you aren't doing yourself a damn bit of good. To think about change without actually changing is quite possibly more idiotic than refusing to consider change in the first place. However, with that said, if you are to give my methods a fair shake, I am sure that you will find great success mixed in with your current approach. I don't expect you to mimic me, I just expect you to take pieces and make them your own. I am not attempting to create little selling clones. I am attempting to create a more intelligent sales force. In turn, I think it will create a much more positive community perception of how a salesperson should act. We don't have to be assholes to sell our products, we just have to be ourselves; I just happen to be a **SALES BADASS**... *are you*?

CHAPTER 1:
DO YOU REALLY
HAVE THE BRASS
FOR THIS JOB?

One of the best things about selling to me is that I have made numerous friends. This isn't because of the number of customers that I have talked to. This is because of the number of bodies that have simply come for the party and got their shit kicked in the process. Being that I am horrible with names I eventually decided that I could no longer call anyone by their name as I just couldn't keep track anymore. I had to start calling everyone by their sales ranking, if they had one at all. If they had no ranking, then they would simply get a generic newbie name such as "new guy" or "lady that likes sweaters". It sounds horrible, but that enabled me to keep enough distance that I wouldn't be upset when someone lost their job and someone always would. I was SO BUSY selling to really give a damn about those who weren't. If they weren't going to stop me from getting yet another plaque, then I honestly didn't give two shits who any of the new folks were.

While I have always been mostly concerned with what is happening with my own sales this doesn't mean that I ignore those that have questions. The problem is that most people regardless of what you say to them are too stubborn to actually use that information. This means that I am constantly wasting my time with people that I don't even have a name for. No matter how many times I attempt to help those around me, they rarely follow the advice. When they do follow it they succeed for a week and go back to their old way of doing things. Unfortunately if their own method was working for them in the first place they wouldn't need to ask me questions and I would sure as hell know their name.

There is a reason why the top salespeople are successful. They are willing to learn. I don't care how long I have been working in the field, I still take advice from other salespeople. I know that I don't have all of the answers so I talk to those around me to see what is working for them. I then take that new knowledge and apply it to what I am already doing to make an even better blend. Top salespeople are always learning, always trying new things, and are more willing to put the extra effort into becoming even better.

The reason why those that aren't in the top aren't successful is because they are whining little bitches. They spend more time complaining and blaming than they do selling or educating themselves on how to sell. The bottom salespeople will typically blame their territories, lead flow, and a variety of other issues as their reason for failing. The people on the top got there because they worked their asses off to get there. They didn't start on the top. It is important that you stop worrying about the politics, stop thinking about what everyone else is doing, and worry about yourself. You are on the bottom because you haven't proven yourself enough to be on the top. You are going to have a shitty territory. You are going to have fewer leads. You are going to get shit assignments. That is part of it. It isn't easy starting out in sales. If it was then nobody would want to do any other job. The key is that you have to take personal responsibility for your shitty sales and realize that you are the reason why they suck. If you can't handle that then try a job where they give you reward stickers and incentive bonuses for doing a good job.

Once you do realize that you are the reason that you are failing and start to achieve things aren't going to magically get better for you. You are going to have to keep doing well. You can't just have one blowout month and expect everything to change. Selling is all about consistency. You have to be consistent because once the month changes you and everyone else is a piece of crap all over again. It doesn't matter if you blew everyone away the month before if you can't replicate it then nobody is going to give a damn. A true salesperson is someone that can get right back into it at the beginning of the next month and pull the same type of numbers that they did the month prior. This is why the top salespeople get the better territories, this is why they get more leads, this is why they get better treatment. They are consistent. They can be relied upon for sales. They are the ones that will ultimately make or break the sales budget. This is the reason why they are pushed harder when sales are tight rather than pushing the bottom rung harder. So if you have aspirations to be on top, you better realize that while your paychecks will get better, you aren't going to work any less.

STARTING OUT

Starting out in sales can be incredibly frustrating. With so much failure it is easy to look at those before you and wonder why they failed. It is easy to get caught up and assume that there is only so much room in the office for success. What you must realize is that there are typically reasons why the people before you failed. Most of the time this is because they simply didn't try hard enough or work smart enough. A lot of times it could also be due to their training.

Part of the reason for so much FAILURE in the industry is because there are so many FAILURES in the industry. I know that may sound like a cool play on words, but it is reality.

With most careers people get into management because they were the best in the position below them. This of course means that those in management SHOULD in theory be the ones that are the most knowledgeable in their career track. Rarely does this model actually apply to the sales world as a whole. Typically, those that are the most successful in sales are making substantially more than those above them leaving little financial incentive to want to change positions. Without the top salespeople moving into the management positions, you are left with a management team that may be great at managing, but probably isn't going to be as strong at TRAINING or RECRUITING. This is one of the major downsides to being new to the sales arena. You are getting your training from people that couldn't hack it in sales themselves. To me, this is a little like sending your child to school every day knowing that their teacher graduated from college with a 'C' average in their area of specialization.

Personally I started out in management and moved to sales when I realized how much money I was losing. This of course was the best move I could have made but by taking myself out of management it would mean finding someone to replace me that was a capable salesperson.   This of course is difficult as most managers once they realize they could be making more in the field will actually make the move and go back to the field. This of course creates an even greater problem for the new salesperson as those around them including those that are supposed to be training them are constantly changing.

It can be very difficult to get into a quality groove when the world around you is always changing but it is important that you realize that you are the single most important factor. You are the one that will ultimately decide your future as a salesperson. So as the world around you changes make sure that you continue to do those things that are working, continue to learn, and constantly strive to be a better salesperson.   In this field you have to rely heavily on yourself for training. Don't expect to learn everything from those around you or above you. Take the initiative, ask questions and read some books. I can never stress how much easier sales can be if you have numerous different approaches that you can use to develop a style that is perfect for you.

KEY TRAITS

While I have been told that salespeople aren't born they are trained numerous times. I really don't believe this. I think it is very obvious that it takes someone with certain personality traits to really be successful. If someone doesn't have these traits they can still have success BUT they are going to be at a huge disadvantage. I think for this reason it is important that you consider the traits of a successful salespeople to determine whether or not you can fit into the role.

CHARISMA

Many have referred to politicians as being charismatic, because they have the ability to appeal to their audience. Someone that is charismatic has the ability to charm those around them. For me it means that you are able to get people to do what you want, because of a natural ability to communicate.

A good example of someone that is charismatic is the stereotypical 'player'. A man that is so good at talking to women that even though they know he is going to 'play' them, he still gets their number and ultimately their heart. Sure that may not be the sweetest charming example of charisma, but I think it gives it generates a common image of what it takes to be charismatic. You should be able to convince someone to do something that they wouldn't readily do. Someone that is charismatic also has a great ability to lead because people listen to them. If you can't do this, then you are going to have a VERY difficult time in sales. People have to be able to make a connection with you in order to trust in what you are saying. If they can't do this, then they are probably going to find someone that they do connect with.

While not all great salespeople are charismatic it is important to realize that even though you may lack the natural ability to influence people you have to find a way to connect with them that draws them in. If you can manage to replicate charisma in a way that is convincing well you may be more charismatic than you think.

DEDICATION

If you want to be good at sales and I mean really good at it, you have to dedicate yourself to it. If you want to be a top salesperson, especially in the beginning, you aren't going to do it by working 40 hours a week. It takes time and effort to develop a funnel of customers. It takes hard work to develop a massive referral base. It takes a lot of practice to learn how to communicate with a variety of different races, with different genders, and different religions.

In sales you should be willing to work until there isn't any work to do. You should be willing to work any day of the week, even weekends. If you aren't as good as your coworkers at selling then working more can help you fill that gap. If you are working more days than your coworkers, if you are more available, then you are going to get more of the 'easier' inbound leads.

A lot of top salespeople get a large enough referral base that they won't work past 5, won't work weekends, don't start before 8,etc. By being flexible and working whenever someone is needed you can BECOME the go to guy for leads when there is a question about availability even if you aren't one of the better closers. This can help you to fill the gap between yourself and the top salespeople.

If you really need a job with a dedicated 40 hours a week you shouldn't be in sales. You need to realize right now that this isn't your typical job. You need to consider yourself on call all of the time. I answer my phone until 10 at night EVERY NIGHT. Why do I do this? Because I know that if I get a call at 9 at night and don't answer that customer could very well call around until they find someone that will. Trust me... there will be someone that will answer that phone. There is nothing shittier than losing a sale because you weren't as dedicated as your competitor. In my industry missing one phone call that would probably take 15 minutes of my night at most would cost me probably $200 in commission on average. In my world, $200 is worth disrupting 15 minutes of my night.

ETHICS

Don't be a piece of shit crap bag! If you are crap bag, then everyone is going to know it. I have seen numerous people that come from selling cars to outside sales and fail miserably. The reason for this is because they are big steaming bags of salesman shit. They will do anything to make a sale and sometimes that is the worst way to make one.

In outside sales you simply can't beat the horse to get the sale. It is so much easier in this job to sell referrals all day long and if you are pissing off your customer base they aren't going to refer anyone except the Better Business Bureau to you. Far too often I find that people in outside sales attempt to generate a problem in order to create a need for their 'remedy'.

A good example would be someone that is selling lawn care products blaming a particular lawn problem on a lawn pest, when they know a lawn pest doesn't exist. This doesn't mean that you can't sell on the future potential for a problem this means that you should NEVER create a problem just for the sake of making a sale. While you may be very successful whether you are ethical or not, this is more about covering your own ass and getting yourself referrals down the road. It is easier to have others work for you, than to work to create all of your own leads.

Some of the best salespeople are shit bags that screw their customers on a daily basis. This doesn't mean you can't be successful as a sack of dog ass it means that you are going to work harder than similarly experienced counterparts to generate each lead that you get.

SELF WORTH

Notice I did not mentioned pricing at all when I discussed ethics. That's because If you are able to sell a product for three times its normal value to a customer sure you may be unethical BUT you are in sales and it is your job to GET THE MONEY. So if you have it so good that you are able to drop numbers like that, go for it. Just realize sometimes the Wal-Mart approach to sales works best.

Selling a shitload of product at a good price will make you more successful than attempting to sell very little for a lot. The more customers you sell, the greater your referral base becomes. This makes selling down the road easier as you aren't going to have to work as hard to obtain quality leads. Someone that sells more customers than their high dollar counterpart is going to work fewer hours long term assuming they both work their referral programs equally. This doesn't mean to low ball, it means to be smart, know your customer and try to sell more product by determining what your customer is willing to spend.

In sales I consider self worth to mean placing a dollar amount on yourself. This means it is your RESPONSIBILITY to make as much as you possibly can, because you are worth that much. This of course can create the ethical problem that I mentioned in the beginning. Should you charge one customer more than another if you have the ability to? The answer should be 'yes'. However, you should always realize that two of your customers may know one another and compare prices. If you charged one considerably more than the other then you better be ready to find a way out of that hole.

There are some products/services that have a flat rate regardless of the customer that you have no control over. However, most of us in sales are going to be selling products/services that we do have a little price flexibility on. If so, then it is your RESPONSIBILITY to make as much as you possibly can! The hard part is that you have to be able to look your customer in the eye and make them truly believe that you gave them a great deal, even when you know you didn't. This doesn't mean charging everyone 3x the rate card. This means that if your rate card says $1100, but you know you can get $1200, it is your RESPONSIBILITY to make as much as you possibly can! Do you notice how I keep stressing this? It isn't always about what the product is worth, it is about what YOU ARE WORTH. So, get what you are worth, and do so with confidence.

Your goal is to leave every single house with the customer feeling as if they got the product/service that they wanted and that they got a great VALUE.

Price is all about perception. If the customer has a perceived value that is positive then you did your job.

PATIENCE

There is nothing in the world worse than a jerk of a salesperson that loses their cool because you aren't signing up for whatever they are selling. I don't care how much time you spend working with someone, you cannot lose your temper. You need to be just as calm and collected with someone you spend 10 minutes with and GET a sale as you are with someone that you spend 5 hours with and DO NOT get a sale. Not only is this the right thing to do it is the best way to generate future referrals.

If you are patient with a customer, assist them in making their decision, and always stay calm there is a huge possibility that while you may not have gotten that same day sale, you could get it down the road unexpectedly. However, if you lose your cool as many salespeople do, then you will NEVER get the sale and you are going to generate HORRIBLE word of mouth at the same time. By being Jeremy Jackson you are not only making your job harder for yourself you are making it harder for the other salespeople that you work with. The worst thing in the world you can do is generate negative word of mouth about your company and your product/service.

I don't give a shit what you have to do in order to calm yourself down you just have to figure out something out so that you constantly remain calm and collected with EVERY customer. This isn't negotiable this is necessity. I don't give a damn about your background. I don't give a damn what you went through growing up. You don't need to be a hot heated idiot all of the damn time. Keep your composure and realize that sometimes shit just isn't going to go your way. The sooner you realize this and learn how to cope with it the better off you will be in sales and in life.

CREATIVITY

This is one of the most important aspects of selling. You could be the best salesperson in the world, but if you aren't able to come up with creative means of generating leads, you probably aren't going to be one of the top salespeople. Someone that closes only 20% of their leads could easily blow away someone that closes 40%. It just comes down to their ability to generate leads. However, the strange thing about seeing more customers is that you are going to eventually become a better closer as well. As you get better, you will slowly begin to sell better. While creativity doesn't seem like a huge deal, it most definitely can be. Your ability to think outside the box could realistically generate enough additional leads that you are able to learn your trade faster, allow you to generate a better pitch, and obviously in time you are going to become a better salesperson. The best part is that as you become a better salesperson if you keep generating creative leads at a faster rate than your coworkers then you are going to find yourself outselling them. I cannot stress enough that if you are able to see more people you have a greater opportunity to make more money and obviously generate more revenue for the company.

As you generate more of your own business you will also open more doors by obtaining a better territory, getting more inbound leads, and of course gaining the respect of your peers. So if you aren't creative you better learn from someone that is if you want to propel yourself to the top of the sales board.

Just because you don't possess all of the above traits doesn't mean that you aren't going to succeed. It is important however that we as salespeople understand just how greatly our personal traits can impact how effective we are in front of the customer. The reason that it is even important to have this section in the book is purely because these are the things that cannot be taught. Being a salesperson is something that you are truly born with. You either have the ability or you do not. I do not entertain the philosophy that you can take someone with no experience or ability to sell and teach them how to sell. There is a big difference between KNOWING and DOING.

I may know everything there is to know about baking, but that doesn't mean that I won't burn a cake every time I try. (this is why I don't bake) This is incredibly true about sales. You could know every closing technique, you could know every detail about the business itself, but at the end of the day if you lack the ability to talk to people you are still going to fail. The important to remember is that even though you aren't the best at selling and that you may not be the absolute best technically as long as you have a natural ability to talk to people then you CAN be successful.

I know I don't have the textbook counter to every objection but I do know how to talk to people. Rather than running from an objection I am able to simply talk to the person as I would like to be talked to and come to the true reason why they objecting. You don't need a textbook education to do this you need only quality social skills. Still I cannot stress enough that if you don't have those social skills you aren't going to be successful in sales.

They key thing to remember is that while it is VERY important to be knowledgeable it is even more important to be likeable. The very first sale that I ever made, I sold without knowing a damn thing about the product that I was selling. I didn't know how to price it. I didn't know how to talk about it. I did however know how to talk to the customer. I was likeable. I sold myself. This doesn't mean that you can simply bullshit your way through life. This does however mean that the customer wants to like you. They want to believe that you are going to resolve their issue, make their life better, do whatever the hell it is that you do and do it well. So, while it is very important to know your product and know it well, CHARISMA is what is going to ultimately get you the sale, especially when you are attempting to sell a product/service that isn't an immediate need.

DRAWBACKS TO SELLING

Unfortunately, there are many people that may be amazing salespeople that just can't deal with the lifestyle of a salesperson. While I personally feel that the lifestyle can be incredibly exciting there are numerous downsides to the career that can really grow old over time. For most of us, we consider this to be a 'sales burnout', which can typically be handled by taking some time away. For others, it isn't always that easy and can be a major reason for them leaving sales altogether. It is because of this, that I think it would be a disservice if I were to simply ignore the negative aspects of selling.

Work Hours

I honestly never know my schedule. I could say that I am going to be done with work by 5 and realize at 9 that I am still working. I could also intend on starting work at 8 every day, but find that I have to work at 6 one day just to accommodate a customer.

The reality is that your income is based on your ability to meet the needs of your customer. If you can't even meet their appointment needs, then they aren't going to entrust you with other more important needs. This typically means that you are at the mercy of your customer on a regular basis. You could also have to work longer hours in order for the office to meet a budget. There have been numerous times when I had to work extra hours or work extra days because the office wasn't making budget, regardless of how well I was doing.

In sales you may work alone but when the office goes to shit you are expected to play with the rest of the team. If you don't have a supportive family, especially your spouse this can become incredibly messy. You have to have someone in your life that is going to support you working a Saturday because the office is behind even if it means you are working EVERY Saturday. This is the sacrifice you make in order to have unlimited earning potential. If your spouse can't understand this and you truly want to be with that person then you may want to consider a different job path. If you are single then you better be ready for a difficult dating life.

Unstable Income

You could make $5 one month or $50,000. Your income can fluctuate so wildly from month to month that at times it becomes impossible to create a true budget. Every salesperson for this reason needs to become a master of their own personal finances. If you don't put aside money for those slower months, then you are going to struggle. There are so many great salespeople that are working part time jobs because they can't get by on the $80k a year that they are making this year, because they budgeted around the $120k they made last year.

You really have to be realistic in your budget or you will starve trying to make up for the shortfalls. I always recommend creating a savings BILL. What I mean by this is that you treat your savings as if it were a bill. This way you are paying your savings account bill rather than pushing the extra money you may have. This method is great because it forces you to recognize that saving should be a priority in this job. The only extra money you have is the money after saving. I normally suggest saving about 20% of your paycheck and whatever else you have leftover at the end of the month push that in as well. Doing this will save you so many problems during your slower months.

As for budgeting always budget around your slowest monthly average. Take the 3 worst months of the last 12 and average them together. This will give you a good RUNNING BUDGET. All of your bills should be based on this. Doing this will ensure that you never RUN OUT of money.

Rejection

This is probably the hardest for most people. **YOU WILL BE REJECTED MORE OFTEN THAN NOT**. If you don't handle rejection well or if you shell up and get depressed by rejection, you will NEVER make it in sales. You are going to get rejected so many times in your career that you aren't even going to show emotion when you are rejected in your personal life. This is probably why salespeople are great bar daters. We are good at getting rejected without giving up. Unfortunately, for many this beats down on them over time. There will be days when you could see 10 people and have every single one reject you. There could be other days when you see 10 people and sell all of them. Sometimes it just doesn't make any sense how things happen, you just have to pick yourself up and move on to the next customer. Personally I take every rejected to be an educational opportunity for myself. If you are constantly getting positive responses, you don't change or grow as a person. If you get rejected, you learn to dig deep and experiment to figure out what will work better. It is through this rejection that you can become a MUCH better salespeople. The trick here is that you have to treat each and every sales opportunity as a learning experience. If you don't sell the customer then you need to find something that you can take from it. You only truly lose out when you don't learn or sell anything with a customer.

- **Groundhog Day** – This is definitely the one thing that I hate the most about selling. No matter how great you were the previous month, you become a piece of crap again the first of every month. You could have been the top salesperson for 200 straight months but it is always going to be about, "what can you do for me this month?" The reality is that you are only as good as what you are currently producing for your company. It doesn't matter how great you were in the past, how awesome you think you may be, or how many pieces of wood/metal you have adorning your walls, you are a piece of crap each and every month until you prove otherwise. This is probably the hardest thing for me to accept. I look at my "I love me wall" on a regular basis looking for motivation, but when it comes to the first of the month, I feel like I have to prove myself all over again. For many, this becomes an obnoxious routine that burns them out. While it may be difficult to do you have to use this as your driving force. You have to be able to turn around month after month with a smile and find a way to pull yourself out of bed ready to tear it up. For me, I was much better at taking it easy the first week and working my ass off the last three weeks of every month. This is what many salespeople do but those months that I was able to give it full energy every day were the months that I had incredible sales. Again, if you are able to work harder than your coworkers and give it your all every day you are going to see more customers and you are going to generate more sales as you become better at selling them.

With all of that said if you think you have the traits to be in sales and you know you can deal with all of the downside bullshit that comes along with it, then good on you. However, if you are reading this and you feel like you are possibly making a huge mistake, then you probably are. I have never experienced any job that chews people up as badly as sales. While I would love to tell you that it is the easiest, most glamorous job in the world, it really isn't. It can be as demanding as it is rewarding. There are weeks when I work 20 hours, then there are weeks when I work 80. There are times when I feel like I can sell anything to anyone and other times when I get worked by the customers and it feels hopeless. You just have to have the brass to pick yourself up and push yourself forward. It is all about staying positive and knowing your real potential. If you are capable of doing that after each and every rejection, then you definitely have stay power.

The goal now that you have decided to move forward should be about making money. If you don't care about money the rest of the book is going to be a huge waste of time as you aren't going to have the motivation to sell. Money is king.

I understand that being materialistic isn't necessarily a positive trait but when it comes to sales you should desire material goods. You should have needs that you would like to fulfill. This doesn't mean that you should focus on them and treat them as a major aspect of your life this means that you have to have a reason to generate more income. If you don't have this desire to make more money then you aren't going to push yourself as hard to be the best. You aren't going to try to sell more when you are already selling more than everyone else. You need to give yourself a reason to push hard even when you are pushing harder than everyone else.

I think it is important to understand that just because I am saying that you should have a material goal doesn't mean that material goal can't be positive in nature. Your goal could be to purchase a larger house, could be to travel the world, or could even be to start a charity. It doesn't matter what that goal is but you need to make it one where the additional money can help you obtain it. For most salespeople this is simple but for some they become so comfortable with mediocrity because they don't have anything that they are striving for. If mediocrity is acceptable don't expect to be the best of the best because you aren't going to be able to force yourself to accomplish more than you need to without a desire for something greater.

CHAPTER 2:
SELLING 'vs'
TRANSACTING

NOTE: I think it is important that you read this section of the book with a VERY open mind. I already know that there are numerous people that would strongly disagree with my statements, but I do believe I provide solid reasoning behind them. This section is purely meant to provoke thought into what it truly means to 'SELL' something.

I have had numerous debates over what a sale actually consists of. I am definitely not Miriam Webster by any stretch of the imagination, but I have come to realize that most people don't truly know what an actual sale is or what it really means to SELL something.

It is of course pretty important if you are in sales to understand what actually constitutes a sale and what doesn't. The idea here is that by better understanding what you are doing with each interaction, you may be able to actually sell more. It also will help to highlight areas of complacency that could be improved upon.

There are two main types of sales. I classify these two types of sales as 'transactions' and of course 'sales'. While they appear to have very different meanings more often than not salespeople and the general public mix the two up. The problem is that by defining what a sale truly is, I know that I am going to annoy those that feel they are salespeople when in reality they are not. To make a sale, you must CONVINCE someone to do something that they wouldn't have done without your assistance. When you are making a TRANSACTION you are assisting someone in making a purchase that they would have made with or without you. This of course is rather simplified so I am going to attempt to illustrate it a little bit further.

TRANSACTION

Customer A walks into a shoe store, knowing that they are going to buy shoes. They get to the salesperson who helps them to purchase the pair of shoes that they came there for. In this example, the salesperson didn't do a damn thing. Just because the title says sales in it doesn't mean that every transaction is a sale. In this example the salesperson is no more of a salesperson than a greeter at Wal-Mart.

SALE

Assume that Customer A from above walks into the same shoe store expecting to buy a pair of shoes that they already had intended to buy but leaves with a slightly better model. This is an IMPROVED SALE. An improved sale is a sale with condition. They wanted shoes but you found them different shoes that just happened to cost more. They still bought what they had intended on buying but you assisted them in purchasing one that was more to their liking. You could have done nothing and let them buy the lower cost shoe but with a little effort you got them to spend more money. So while this is an improved sale you didn't completely sell the customer.

To really sell this customer would mean to get them to purchase socks, shoelaces, polishes, etc. Those are items they never intended on purchasing when they walked into the store. While the IMPROVEMENT counts as selling to some extent it is far more impressive to sell the customer something that they didn't want in the first place. To do this you are using your skill and knowledge of the customer's needs in order to convince them to your way of thinking. They may have needed these items anyway but by anticipating their needs you sold them on it. This is what it takes to truly make a sale.

To better understand the concept of an IMPROVED SALE I am going to attempt to break it down a bit further. The reason a customer wanted their original choice may have simply been because they were ignorant to what they ultimately purchased. The customer may not have known that this item existed and if they had they may have chosen it all on their own without any assistance. If this is the case then no sale was truly made and it would merely be an improved sale since the act of suggestion by the salesperson got them to make the change in purchase. Still the salesperson got the customer to do something that they may not have done without the suggestion. So even though it is an improved sale and not a true one it is important nonetheless.

The difference between a sale, an improved sale, and a transaction is the effort involved. Anyone can sell someone a product that they already intended on buying. It takes a salesperson to sell them something else. If they didn't plan on purchasing socks and you sell socks, you just made more money for the company and made a sale that wouldn't have been made otherwise. This is the reasoning for having salespeople in a store rather than simple allowing the customer to run around all willy nilly grabbing whatever the hell they want. A salesperson is meant to improve upon what normally would be sold and suggest other items to increase the overall purchase by each customer.

The reason why all of this is important to understand is that far too many people feel that they are salespeople when in reality they are not. They may have the title of salesperson, but if they aren't upgrading or selling people products they didn't intend on buying, they aren't selling them a thing, they are assisting them in a transaction.

Another example would be If you worked in an appliance store and a customer tells you that they are looking for an economical refrigerator and you sell them one. You did a great service for that customer, but you didn't sell them anything. You assisted them in making a transaction. If you convinced them to buy the refrigerator with the DVD screen in the door, that would be an improved sale. However, if someone comes in looking for a top of the line refrigerator and you sell them the one with the DVD screen in the door, you didn't make a sale, you made a transaction. In order for it to truly be a SALE, you have to actually get the customer to do something that they didn't originally intend on doing such as buying a warranty. If you really want to prove that you are a salesperson however you should not only get them to buy the upgraded refrigerator but something to go along with it. When you get someone to buy a refrigerator when they wanted a refrigerator even an upgraded one you may be selling them an upgrade but you aren't convincing them to do something much different than they would have done on their own. To sell them an accessory or warranty to go with it would be a true sale. The idea is that as a salesperson you should not only be able to get the improved sale but be able to sell them something outside of what they had intended on buying along with it.

The same is true in outside sales. If someone calls your office looking to get lawn care and you sell them lawn care, congratulations, you assisted them in making a transaction. Anyone could have done it, good job on being that 'anyone'. Your goal shouldn't be to simply do what the customer wants you to do. Your goal should always be to go above and beyond. You need to give them reason to spend more money than they originally planned on spending while making them feel good about doing it at the same time. If you can do this,

---

then you are a salesperson. If you aren't able to do this then you probably aren't going to last very long in outside sales. Unfortunately, the large majority of the transactions done in outside sales are going to be ones where you have to convince someone to buy things they never intended to buy in the first place. It isn't a matter of upgrading them it is a matter of getting them to buy **SOMETHING** in general.

Most every sale that someone in outside sales makes is going to be one where the customer didn't intend on spending a dime. This is what makes outside sales so difficult, but it is also why we are paid so much better than those that simply sit in a store and wait for customers. We have to not only convince the customer to make an appointment with us we have to convince them that they want to spend money they probably didn't intend on spending. For most of us that means convincing someone that didn't intend on spending any money to potentially spend thousands of dollars. This isn't an easy task. It takes someone with a lot of grit and determination to ask for this much money from someone that never intended on spending it in the first place.

I got used to asking for large sums of money while working in auto sales. While I felt like I learned a lot about closing a sale, getting to the real objection, and all of the other stereotypical sales bullshit, I wasn't really selling anything. The customers that ended up on the car lot were there because they typically wanted to buy a car now or in the relative future. So while I made numerous sales, I was selling them something that they came to buy.

This doesn't mean that selling cars is easy, because it most definitely is not. It just means that while it was difficult to get the customer to make the purchase, I wasn't truly SELLING them unless I got them to buy a more expensive version of the vehicle they intended on buying, got them to buy extra services, or got them to upgrade their equipment. Sure selling cars is one of the first things that anyone thinks of when it comes to sales, but there is far more transacting going on than actual selling.

I can't tell you how many times I had a customer come in and tell me that they wanted to buy a specific type of car, with a specific package, and that they wanted this warranty, they wanted these stripes, or whatever. The customer comes in and pretty much tells the salesperson everything that they would like to do. This of course is transacting. There were many times the customer wasn't sure what they wanted and I had to assist them in finding the correct vehicle. In these instances I didn't really sell them either. They never gave me any limitations. They never gave me an opportunity to upgrade them. Without this, you aren't truly making a sale, you are assisting them in making a transaction. While it is substantially different than the customer telling you what they want, I still didn't have to convince them to do something they wouldn't typically do.

This is what makes selling so difficult. The hard part is admitting to yourself when you are truly selling and when you are simply transacting. The key is to make sure that you make at least one sale with every transaction that you may do. If you do this, you can turn every transaction into a sale. This is what separates a salesperson from the lady working the counter at a shoe store. Just because you work in a car dealership and you have title of car salesman doesn't mean you are any better at selling than the lady at the camera counter in your local retailer. What makes the difference is when you are able to get that little bit extra and convince the customer to do just a little bit more. That is selling.

While I think the above statements may make a lot of those in traditional sales angry, I do have a strong argument for my case. In car sales and in other traditional sales, you are selling yourself more than you are selling the product/service. This is because most of the time the customer is coming to you with a desire to purchase a particular item. When it comes to cars, they may be shopping around for price and service, however, they are mostly looking to find a salesperson that seems to truly care about their needs. Your goal is to become that person. If you are able to sell yourself in traditional sales, then often times the product will sell itself. This is because the product itself was sold prior to the customer walking in. You just had to find a way to convince the customer that you are the one that they want to work with.

If the customer buys something they aren't intending on buying then that changes everything, but you must realize something brought that customer into the dealership and that was their need to purchase a car. What you get them into doesn't ultimately matter unless you are able to push the limitations that they put on you. If they tell you that they will not spend more than $10,000 and you get them to spend $15,000 that is selling. If the customer tells you that they want the base model and you get them to purchase the limited edition super loaded mega awesome model that would also be a sale. These would both be IMPROVEMENT SALES but they would be sales nonetheless.

What it all comes back to is your ability to get the customer to do that little bit extra. If this means buying an extra key fob, buying new floor mats, a warranty package, or whatever the hell else you get them to buy you are getting them to do just a bit more. If you are able to do this with each and every customer no matter what you are selling you will know that you are truly a salesperson and you aren't just transacting.

Outside sales is a different beast altogether. You are forced to sell people things that they didn't think they wanted or needed. This of course is going to be your daily routine. You are going to see more customers that didn't originally want what you are offering more often than you will see people that wanted your product/service. So when you sell things in outside sales, you are truly selling not only yourself but the product as well. I think this is a major reason why those that typically work in car sales, inside sales, or other types of sales typically fail miserably when they come to outside sales. Outside sales forces you to be far more creative in your selling than you would be otherwise. The perceived need is created by the salesperson, rather than the customer already having that need when they walk into a store. Rarely do you have desire for a product prior to your interaction. You must create desire, you must create the value, and you must sell everything, including yourself.

Another major issue with outside sales is that the traditional methods of closing the sale don't always apply. Many times in you will find yourself in a person's home or place of employment. This is their comfort zone and if you attempt to use aggressive sales strategies on them they are going to ask you to leave. When you are selling a car, they are in your house. You can be aggressive because it is your house. You know that they came there to buy something and have to get to the reason that they aren't and close out the deal. In outside sales, the reason they aren't buying could be simply because they don't give two shits about what you are offering.

If the traditional approach worked then you wouldn't be reading this book right now. I am not a traditional salesperson and I realize that there is nothing traditional about outside sales. This is an area of sales that is absolutely brutal and as such you have to keep an open mind. You have to be able to learn with every sale that you make or lose. If you came from another type of sales it will be even harder but if you dedicate yourself to the process and learn to trust your natural instinct you'll be able to find success even when it seems impossible.

The goal of this section of course is that you will now look at every sale a little differently. Look at each and every sale as an OPPORTUNITY. You may know that the customer wants product A, but you have OPPORTUNITY to sell them product B along with it. They already know they are going to spend enough for product A, so why not work a little bit harder and assume the challenge of getting them to also purchase a complimentary product. If your customer is already sold on a particular price sometimes it can be easier to get them to pay just a little bit more to get additional products/services. Your goal should be to get them to understand the important of this extra purchase and push the value of it.

If nothing else, I want you to realize that it is a whole lot easier to work smarter than harder. I know that is incredibly trite, but it so true that I can't say it any other way. If you sell more to each customer, then you aren't going to have to sell as many customers. Again, this is trite, but it is the whole idea of doing more with less. These phrases are important to remember, because they are what separate the top tier salesperson from the middle tier and the middle tier from the bottom. These phrases are overused for a reason. They are true. Keep them in mind every time you close out a deal to maximize your overall sales potential.

CHAPTER 3 :

IT IS ABOUT TIME YOU GREW A PAIR!

𝓟robably the most important trait that any salesperson can possess is CONFIDENCE. If you are a timid little sack of a salesperson your customer is not only going to walk all over you, they probably aren't going to trust you either. If a customer can't trust you then they probably aren't going to want to give you money. Sure they may love your personality but if you look nervous, sound nervous, or act as if you are hiding something your customer will perceive this as uncertainty. They are going to wonder if you are trying to shoot air up their ass. Sure some customers may bite on this pathetic salesperson approach but most are going to wonder if your lack of confidence stems from your lack of knowledge or a shady product or service. You have to understand that everything that you do could create a perception in the customers mind about you whether it be positive or negative. Your goal obviously is to create nothing but positive thoughts while eliminating all of the negative ones.

Everything that you say or do will be judged by your customers. If you spit when you talk they are going to assume that you lack manners. If you stutter/stammer frequently they are going to assume that you lack confidence in the product/service you are offering. If you say, "uhh" or "umm" more than you say anything else, they are going to assume that you are searching for answers and buying time. These things as well as looking everywhere but at the customer, wringing of the hands, twitching, etc... all make you look incredibly nervous about what you are selling and gives off a hugely negative perception that you are nervous or hiding something. If you can't appear confident in front of your customers, you are going to cost yourself numerous sales. I don't give a damn how great your pitch is or how well your brochure presentation may be, if you aren't able to do it while looking your customer in the eyes, you are going to look like you are full of shit.

For me, confidence is paramount. When I go to purchase a car for example, I want the person that runs up to me, is excited to make the sale and puts in that extra effort. I want them to be able to look me dead in the eye when they feed me their bullshit lines. I know they are bullshit, but I want them to be confident about it. If they are, then I will keep working with them. If they aren't, then I am going to request that I have a better bullshitter. This doesn't mean that you need to lie to make a sale, but it does mean that you need to present every product/service that you have as if it is the greatest product known to man. I know it isn't the greatest product/service without even knowing what it is and I'm sure you know it too, but if you don't give off the appearance that this product makes you sweat in excitement just thinking about it, you could cost yourself the sale. I don't care if you are selling the benefits of crushed ice during the coldest time of year in Alaska, you better make it appear like owning this ice is so cool that the customer would be less of a person without it. If you can get them excited about this ice or plunger or bag of monkey farts then you are going to get them closer to making the sale. Unfortunately, this is where most salespeople fail miserably. You could have been in this situation a thousand times before but you still shake and look around like it was your first time. Maybe it is time you stop being timid and learn to grow a pair!

EYE CONTACT

One of the biggest things that I notice with salespeople is that they try TOO HARD to be confident. As a sales manager, I stressed confidence more than anything else, so they would attempt to show me their confidence by giving the customer the stare down. The problem is that they wouldn't blink their eyes and would come off more creepy than confident. Eye contact is very important, but it doesn't mean you can't blink your eyes or look elsewhere every now and then. It just means that you should look at the customer on a regular basis and really appear as if you give a damn about what they are saying. This forces you to listen to their needs, it assists you in determining what they are thinking, and it shows that you aren't a confidence lacking pansy ass.

The key thing to remember is that when you have two or more people in the room, try to position yourself so that you can look over at all of them at the same time. If you position yourself in the middle, then you are going to be constantly turning your head to give them equal attention. This is especially important when you are talking to a husband and wife. If you give the wife too much attention, you could give off the appearance that you have a physical interest in her. If you give the man too much attention then you could give off the appearance that you assume he is in charge and vice versa if you are a woman. If you are giving a commercial presentation, then it is important that you give attention to everyone, but the person with the most authority needs to get the majority of it. Keep in mind, this is the person that is going to be making the ultimate decision so they need to be given the respect that they deserve. As a special note, by being in the middle and turning your head side to side you are psychologically telling them no. While I don't necessarily believe that this is going to ultimately impact your sale I do believe that you shouldn't be stupid enough to sit in the middle.

One of the biggest issues with eye contact when I would work with my salespeople is that they would attempt to give me a look that looked more seductive than serious. I never understood why people have such major issues simply looking at someone. Just look at them like you would an orange or a dog or a refrigerator. You aren't trying to make-out with them you are simply trying to convey that you are paying attention even if you really don't give a damn. Just make sure that you blink and look normal and you should be alright. If you notice you are looking at them the same way that you do your significant other then you are either seducing your customer or giving a less than appealing look to your partner. Either way something is wrong so now that you realize it, fix it.

BODY MOVEMENT

If you are someone that is constantly fidgeting like myself you are going to have another battle. I personally make incredible eye contact both in sales and in my personal life. My biggest issue is that I struggle with controlling my desire to move my body and wiggle around like a 5 year old with a sugar high in a ball pit filled with candy. Luckily, I have found ways to get around this. If you move your feet around a lot, you really don't have much to worry about as you should be sitting down at a table when you are talking to your customers anyway. If this is the case, your feet are hidden. However, if you happen to have a glass table, try wrapping your legs together and this should prevent you from flailing wildly and should create only a mild movement that the customer most likely won't even think twice about.

If you are the type that moves your hands frequently like myself, then you should consider keeping a pen in your hands at all times. To control my need to move my hands, I find that I draw a lot of pictures and diagrams for my customers. This not only controls their attention and draws them in to what I am trying to say, but it allows me to move my hands without looking like a freak. The idea is that rather than making yourself uncomfortable, use the tools that you have at your disposal to turn it into your presentation.

If you a hair twirler you have another battle. Hair twirling is associated with the ditzy. Just because you twirl your hair doesn't make you an idiot but it is going to be a distraction to your customer and could potentially make them wonder if you are telling them the truth. Just like any other hand movement attempt to keep something in your hand. Draw pictures like I do. The more I find the need to move my hands or body around the harder I work on using my pen to tell the story of what I am attempting to sell. If I want a customer to think about a price then I keep circling it over and over again. This may serve to keep my hands busy but it could also get the customer to make a decision faster as they are now focusing on that decision and not so much on the world around them.

If you are a lip smacker, bubble blower, or pen chomper I really have no good advice for you other than tossing some mints in your mouth a couple minutes before the sale so that they have time to dissolve. If nothing else this may give you less of a desire for mouth play and hopefully you can control yourself a bit.

VERBAL COMMUNICATION

I shouldn't really have to stress how important the verbal aspect of communication is but for some reason I find myself preaching about it more and more frequently. You have to realize that the tone itself and how loud you are can really impact whether your customer is going to listen to you or not. If you have a deep authoritative voice, you are going to sound like you have a greater understanding of your products/services and will sound more confident without even trying. If you have a lighter voice, you may sound more charming/caring. The goal should be to present yourself in a caring manner, but give yourself enough tone to your voice that you sound confident as well. This is much easier for men to do as our voices are naturally deeper. However, women are much better at coming off as sincere in what they say. I'm not saying that every man should sound like Barry White or that all women should take up smoking to get a nice raspy man voice. I am saying that you should firm up your voice and be able to project it in a manner that demands attention. If you were to listen to the audio of some of the most famous speakers you would realize just how important the tone of their voice is. You aren't going to find any speakers that have a pitchy voice or one that is scratchy. You are going to find that they are going to have a smooth, rhythmic, powerful tone to them.

A while back I had a salesperson who knew how to sell, was good at doing everything that related to making the sale, but he had some issues with speaking to customers. His major issue was that he would talk very quietly. This is how he naturally spoke and while he was definitely confident in himself and the product, anyone that didn't know him would have assumed that he was nervous. I began to work with him on a regular basis, because I knew that once he got past this he was going to start closing substantially more business. So, each and every morning when he came to the office, I made him speak to me with his 'big boy' voice. In fact, it got to the point where I wouldn't even acknowledge him until he spoke loud and firm. The goal of course was to give him the confidence in using that louder voice so that he could start using it while speaking with customers. It also made for some excellent personal entertainment in the beginning as it was incredibly awkward sounding. With time, he began to speak loud enough where customers could understand him without stepping out of his comfort zone.   This of course led to much better sales because the customer wasn't afraid that they misheard something.

PULLING IT TOGETHER

One thing that I always told my salespeople is that they have to walk into the room as if they have the biggest balls/ovaries in that room. Not sure why this makes the concept easier to understand but apparently it does. The idea is that you should be the one that sets the tone of the conversation. If you walk up to the customer and they start dictating how everything is going to go they are going to have a lot easier time telling you no. However, if you take control from the beginning you are the one that is going to have control when it comes to closing out the sale. The person that is the most confident is going to be the one that has the upper hand. I sort of think of it like training a dog. If you go into a room and you are scared a dog is going to sense that and typically will try to show its dominance. However, if you are to walk into a room and assume the role of the alpha then typically the dog is going to respect that and back down without a challenge. If you walk in and you give no appearance of confidence or the lack thereof that dog will probably still test the boundaries a bit to see where they stack up. Your goal should be the alpha from the start in order to control the direction and ultimate outcome of each and every sales call.

One of the easiest ways to show your confidence is through the assumption of a sale. If you are to walk into the house like someone would be stupid to not purchase your product or service then it will make the customer start to think they are missing out by not having this product or service. Use every type of communication to draw them in. Use your hands by starting at eye level and drawing your hands slowly down to your excellent plasticware set. Show them that you had the NUMBER 1 product in your industry for the last 10 years. Point at them and let them know THEY are right. Give them a firm nod with eye contact to let them know that you are paying attention to each and every word. Throw those eye brows around a bit show them that you are intrigued, amazed, or delighted by what they are saying. Draw a couple of pictures just to appear like you are that much more prepared and to prove to yourself that you DO have control over your own body. Tell them with authority how great your product is and have them actually believe you. Doing all of these things while making statements that show that you assume they are going to purchase will get you that much closer to the sale. Use statements such as :

"What general time of year would be best for you to take this vacation?"
"What types of things would you be cooking with this top of the line kitchen set?"
"I hope you plan on inviting me over for dinner after purchasing these cookbooks!"

With each of the statements above I assumed that they are going to purchase what I am selling before we ever got to the closing table. I appeared so confident in the product/service that it would appear that I would be surprised if they were to tell me no. Not to mention after they answer the question they are giving me a commitment to go on vacation during the summer, make shrimp scampi, etc. This of course could always be used later if you are eventually told no. You could bring it back up and say something along the lines of "So does this mean you aren't going to invite me over for shrimp scampi now?" By doing this you brought yourself back in for a last ditch opportunity for a sale in a pleasant manner without having to push the product on someone. This is typically where I use pricing power to gain the sale. Ask them how much it would be worth to them knowing the full retail value to be able to create incredible meals. To go on a fabulous vacation. To do whatever else you may have discussed. You can only do this if you were confident enough to assume the sale from the beginning.

In selling, assuming the sale is one of the easiest ways to show that you are confident in your product/service. If you walk up to a house and use statements such as, "when we start your service", or any other sale assumptive statement you are telling the customer that you are there to get their business and that you are used to hearing 'yes'. Customers don't want to think that they are the only customer that you have ever sold. They want to be one of the sheep. They want to be just like everyone else on the block. If you sold all of their neighbors, they want to be part of that group. However, if your competitor sold all of their neighbors and they are the one that is picking you, they are going to start to wonder why everyone else went a different direction. So it is very important that you give off the impression that it would be 'strange' if they didn't choose you without coming off as arrogant.

There is a big difference between being confident and arrogant and unfortunately many people tend to blend the two together. If you are confident, you are confident without saying it. If you are arrogant, you are confident but you make it known. For example, someone that is arrogant is going to say things like, "of course you are going to do business with me", "we are simply the best", "it would be a mistake to choose anyone else", etc. If you are confident without being arrogant, these things should be said without saying them. You should be able to command that attention that you deserve from the start, you should be able to assume the sale by talking about what you WILL be doing for the customer, and then actually getting the sale.

DO NOTS OF CONFIDENCE

- **DO NOT...** talk about how bad the competition is and how amazing you are in comparison.
- **DO NOT...** talk about how someone's friends/neighbors made a mistake in choosing the competition over you.

- **DO NOT...** talk about your accomplishments within the company or in your personal life. Nobody wants you to brag about how great or amazing you think you are. Talk about the customer, let them talk. The more you talk, the better chance you have of blowing the sale. Keep in mind you still need to control the conversation by guiding them in what they say.

The DO NOTS are arrogance, not confidence. This is an excellent way to lose a sale to your competition. Take the high road, talk about your own company, and if you must talk about the competition, then do so in a way that allows you to compare yours to theirs. Comparing apples to apples is sometimes the best way to convince a customer to your side when all else fails. It also shows that you did your research and gives you reason to be so confident in what you are selling. If you can back up what you are saying, you are going to look more like an expert in your field than a salesperson and that is going to get you far more sales in the long run.

CHAPTER 4 :
STEREOTYPISTS
TYPE TO A BEAT

It is amazing how the stupidest of things can effect perception. If someone is wearing a cowboy hat, most would assume that person listens to country music. If someone has tattoos, they are probably a rocker or do drugs. Sure these are stereotypes, but they are stereotypes for a reason. People wouldn't automatically make these assumptions unless there was truth to them on a relatively large scale. Sure this means that I have to live with white guys not being able to jump or dance, but when I truly think about it, I really suck at dancing and honestly I can't jump as high as many of my non-white friends. The problem in sales is that these stereotypes are going to be what the customer sees when meeting you for the first time. It is because of this that it is so important that you give them a solid reason to alter their perception.

Perception with your customer isn't going to be based purely on race. I find that customers are going to judge you based on your race, weight, age, the way that you talk, eye contact, how you dress, and numerous other things. It is important that we as salespeople at least understand what we are being judged on so that we can determine how to attempt to alter that perception. By allowing the perception to stand, we risk losing a sale based purely on the inability of the customer to get past their misconceptions of who we are. If the customer sees my spiky hair, my facial hair, my piercings, and tattoos and assumes I do drugs, but they are strongly against those that do drugs, I could lose that sale. However, if I understand many people will have this misconception about my appearance I can cover up my tattoos, remove my piercings, shave a bit, and control my hair, then the customer could see me completely different.

IMAGE IS EVERYTHING

When people say, 'image is everything', they must be talking about salespeople. It sounds very materialistic, but in sales it truly is about what you have. If you are in outside sales and you drive up to someone's house in a beat up 30 year old car, you are going to lose a lot of trust. Sure this might play well if your customers are in a similar situation, but it isn't going to play well with your more affluent customers. In fact, if you pull up in a beat up car, you may be judged by the middle to upper class in a very negative manner. They aren't going to be as trusting of you, because of the negative perception of the lower class. Unfortunately, many people are going to assume that you are going to be more prone to steal things from their homes and take advantage of them, because that is the perception of lower class people. However, if you pull up in luxury vehicle you may give off the impression that you are super successful because you are 'too good'. Most are going to assume that you didn't get to where you are by giving the best price in town. They are going to assume you got that vehicle by ripping a lot of people off with your incredibly high prices. Altering this perception is as easy as purchasing a reasonable vehicle for the job that you do. If you want a luxury car, consider one that doesn't have a high mental price tag attached to it. Instead of a BMW, buy a high end Toyota, Ford, Chevy, Etc. You could even buy a truck. The idea is that most people know so little about BMW that they assume that all of their vehicles, regardless of their actual price tag are high priced luxury vehicles. The same is true with Mercedes. If you have a vehicle with this high price tag perception or one that is beat up, try parking it out of eye shot so that you aren't judged by it.

You must always be aware of your image in sales. You should know that wearing jeans and a polo isn't going to work as well for commercial business as it would for residential clientele. So it is important to really base your dress on the type of customer you intend on seeing each day. If your customer base consists of all upper class people, then you can pretty much dress, drive, and act like them. If you have a mix however, then you need to take that into consideration. You may be making upper class dollars, but you have to dress and drive like you are middle class if you want to appeal to both. By driving an efficient newer model vehicle, you will show the upper class that you driving an intelligent vehicle for what you do, while the lower class will assume that you are doing alright, but you aren't making a fortune either. The goal is to look successful without appearing to be overly so. The best plan of attack is to simply wear a company uniform and drive a company vehicle, but when those aren't available, you have to present yourself in a manner that is respectable to all classes of people.

Typically I try to plan my appearance around those I will be seeing throughout the day. If I am going to be seeing commercial customers, I want to give the appearance of success, so I will probably drive my Nissan 350z, wear a quality polo shirt without company branding, some nice dress shoes and bring my state certification with me as identification around my neck. If I am going to see a typical customer, I am probably going to drive my Kia Spectra, wear a company polo shirt, and some simple brown dress shoes.

The thing to keep in mind is to dress the part. You wouldn't wear a suit to the gym. The same goes for sales. Don't wear something that isn't going to be appropriate for that particular audience. This doesn't mean that you have to spend a great deal of money in order to accommodate everyone. It is just important to realize that every bit of the way you look and act can determine the opinion that is generated about you.

OVERCOMING NATURE/CULTURE

One of the most difficult aspects of selling is selling to people that are not like our own. I have heard countless times people complaining about how they hate selling to 'Asians' or 'Middle

Easterners' or 'Indians' or whatever. The problem isn't as much them as it is YOU. It is your bias that is keeping you from selling to them not their genetic disposition to not buy from you. I think far too often we blame race as a reason for not getting a sale. The problem is that by doing this, we are giving up on a lot of potential customers. Some may have a negative impression of your race it is up to you to prove them wrong while at the same time overcoming your own negative perceptions.

Selling to different races/cultures can be one of the easiest things that you could possibly do, once you know how to do it. For myself, I learned how to sell to other races/cultures quickly because I had a sales territory that was mostly Indian/Korean. While I already had the common misconceptions about them being hard negotiators, I went into the appointments with an open mind. I wasn't expecting sales, I was expecting an education. This is paramount to growing as a salesperson. When you know that you are in a situation that you probably aren't going to get a sale, you should always come back with something. For me, this was the education on how to sell to this type of customer. I knew that if I couldn't sell to them, I was going to at least leave their home with an idea of how to sell them in the future.

What I found was that by simply talking to them the same way I would talk to anyone of my own race/culture, I could obtain all the information out needed to make the sale. Many times when we are confronted with people that are different than us, we are afraid to probe and ask questions, but that is EXACTLY what you should do. I started saying things such as, "I notice the accent a bit, where is that from?" The idea is to get them to talk about their 'home' country. However, you have to be smart when you do this. Don't ever assume that you know where somebody is from and don't say that when the person clearly doesn't have an accent. Just because they are of Korean decent, doesn't mean that they have ever been to Korea. So don't make assumptions, always probe to find out the answer. When you get people talking about themselves and what they are passionate about the walls are quickly torn down and what goes from being a business transaction becomes something much more cordial. The best part is that the more you learn about these people and their culture the easier it will be in the future. Just keep in mind that you should NEVER talk about politics with a customer unless you know that your opinion directly matches theirs. This is also true with other controversial topics. I recommend however avoiding controversial conversations altogether as they are unpredictable. This could turn out very poorly as many people get very passionate about the politics of their birth country. The goal should always be to keep things educational. Get them talking, give them good eye contact, and show them that you are interested in what they have to say, even if you aren't.

The main thing to keep in mind is that regardless of where people come from, most enjoy the opportunity to talk about themselves and their family. It is up to you to initiate conversation that will ultimately cause them to open up. If you don't, they are most likely never going to volunteer that information.   As they open up, you should too. By opening up to the customer you are giving them more reason to trust you. They may not trust Richard Ramsey but they may trust the father Richard Ramsey.

The rewards to establishing these relationships with other cultures can be huge. I get more referrals from my Indian customers than from any other group. The reason is because I talk to them like people, not like they are just another sale. In my industry I have yet to see a single Indian salesperson. As such, those people that are willing to take the extra time and communicate with them are going to be the ones that not only get that sale, but will probably get the sales of their family members as well. Unlike many Caucasian families many other cultures are VERY close to one another. They have tight family ties and typically have strong relationships within their own communities as well. So when you sell one person you may very well be setting yourself up for a huge funnel of constant referrals from that community.

Just like our perceptions of the customer, you have to consider how you are perceived when you meet with your customer for the first time. The worst thing in the world would be for you to come off as a complete D-Bag from the beginning. This would have obvious negative ramifications when attempting to close the deal. The way that you are perceived is going to be different based on who you are talking to at any given time. The main thing to remember is that as long as you are respectful, make good eye contact, give equal attention to all parties, then you should be fine. In many cultures the male is dominant, so if they push to control your attention, give them that attention. You should always attempt to be the sales person that they want you to be. So if that means you have to take off your shoes when you normally wouldn't, you should accommodate that. If it means that you need to sit with your legs crossed because they are, you should probably attempt to do that as well. Just make sure that you aren't trying to BE THEM. If they talk in a certain manner, just talk how you normally would. Don't attempt to have an accent because they have one. If you have a sister in law that is from their culture, don't bring it up unless they ask. If someone from another culture were to tell me that they have a white sister in law, whether it is true or not, I would see it as a sign of kissing my ass and buttering me up. I can only assume that other cultures see it the same way. Now if the customer says that they were born in a particular city then you can state that your sister in law is from there. However, it is important that you know a little bit about that area before you do this. The customer will almost always ask for more information and if you don't know the details they might assume that you don't care enough about their culture to even listen to your sister in law.

TATTOOS AND PIERCINGS

If you have tattoos you may want to consider covering them up. I know that tattoos are meant to be an expression of who you are, but honestly the customer doesn't give a damn about your flair for body art. They are looking for someone that is going to be professional, tell them about the products/services your company offers, and get the hell out. Having exposed tattoos and piercings can be somewhat taboo for many in a professional situation. By exposing these you may have great luck selling to others with similar interests, but you are going have a more difficult time selling to older generations in many cultures. Even for someone like myself that has tattoos and has had piercings, I would be more apt to trust someone that is clean cut and covered up. Someone that has tattoos and piercings is just going to have to work harder to make the sale if they choose to keep them exposed.

You should also consider the distraction of tattoos and piercings. While it can at times assist in creating dialog with those that have an interest in them, most of the time it doesn't. What you will typically find is that the average person either doesn't like you because of them or they are going to focus on the tattoos and piercings. If they lose focus on you and what you are saying, then it doesn't matter how good of a salesperson you are, it will be very difficult to pull them back in and ultimately make the sale.

It is far easier to simply cover your tattoos and remove your piercings than it is to attempt to make up for them. I really don't care how much you paid for your body art or how important it is to you, cover it up. I have a tattoo myself and I have had numerous piercings throughout my life. Sure it is great when people notice what you have done to your body. The problem is that more often than not the people that are going to notice aren't going to appreciate it as much as you do. If everyone loved tattoos and piercings, then everyone would have them. When you are attempting to gain the trust and confidence of a customer it is NOT the time to attempt to make a statement. You aren't going to change popular opinion in regards to body art by yourself, so do what you have to do to look professional and get the sale.

I have seen a lot of people that have been incredibly stubborn on this and I really don't understand why. It is your job to get the sale. By attempting to be the God of all that is body art, you are only making your life that much more difficult. Accept that society doesn't value your art as much as you do and move on.

RELIGION

Religion is the destroyer of sales. I cannot explain this in a more blasphemous way but it is true. I know that my mother and a great majority of my friends will probably disagree with this statement and this entire section, but it needs to be addressed. This is probably the most important section of this entire book. To ignore it purely because of a close religious affiliation is self destructive. I assure you that I have good basis for my statements.

All of us have our belief system. Some of us have recently discovered these beliefs while others have had these beliefs deeply engrained in everything that they are since birth. The major issue isn't religion/beliefs in general but the number of belief systems that exist. So many of these beliefs conflict with one another which is a major reason why there is so much religious conflict in the world. These conflicts create such an emotional response that wars have been started because of these beliefs. If you look back through history you will see that religion drives many people. This is what has started numerous wars. It has resulted in mass executions. It is a major worldwide conflict. They key is that you don't attempt to get involved in it. This has been a battle that different religions have been waging for centuries. You aren't going to change these beliefs in a single sales call. If you can let me know where I can buy your book as you sure as hell are better than I am.

In sales, you truly need to be neutral when it comes to religion. I hate the concept of hiding who you are just to appease others, but when it comes to religion you definitely need to tone it down considerably. I am not saying that you can't pray before every sales call. I am not saying that you can't be proud of your background and beliefs. What I **am** saying is that you shouldn't be walking around with your 10 pound Jesus cross dangling around your neck. I **am** saying that you shouldn't walk up to the door and immediately make religious statements or even close the transaction in that manner. You may normally say "god bless" after ever sale, but this can be offensive to some people. I know I personally feel uncomfortable when someone says it to me. I feel obligated to say something in return but since I am not religious I don't know what the hell I am supposed to say that respects my beliefs while still acknowledging theirs. I think it is important to keep this in mind, because I personally would take this as a negative even though the majority of the religious population may see this as a positive. I think a good alternative would be to simply say, "have a blessed day". You are basically saying the same thing, but you earn the respect from your religious core while not offending the non religious.

When you talk about religion to someone that doesn't have the same religious affiliation as you do, you are going to sound like you are preaching. The honest truth is that those that don't have your same beliefs don't give a damn about your church, they don't care about your awesome religious text, and they really don't want to hear your religious mouth noise. They have their beliefs, they aren't the same as yours, get over it! Again, this doesn't mean that you can't believe. It just isn't a good idea when you are at a sales call to open your mouth about it. This is especially true when you are talking to those that aren't religious at all. Talking religion to someone that is non-religious is like talking to a girl about peeing standing up. Sure they are capable of talking about it, but honestly they really don't know where the hell you are coming from. They may still listen to you out of common courtesy but I assure you they are waiting for a moment where they can escape.

Now, if you are lucky enough to be religious and go to a house where they obviously come from the same background as you, excellent! Those that are extremely devout are much more likely to do business with a believer than they would with someone that is a non-believer. By sharing this information with someone with the same affiliation you give yourself a lot of breathing room. You are now able to build trust based upon your beliefs alone. Sure your presentation may have been amazing, but having that personal connection with the customer sometimes means far more to them than anything that came out of that hole in your face.

Religion isn't a bad thing! I think it is important that people have something to believe in. The key is that you have your beliefs while respecting the beliefs of your customers. They really don't want to hear about something that goes against everything that they believe in. It would be the same as someone inviting me into their home and then I decide to toss bags of shit at their children. Sure I may think it is fun but they probably will not. I know that may appear to be a little bit extreme, but religion runs VERY DEEP for many people. If you cross that line when it comes to religion it is almost impossible to step back behind it. This just goes back to the previous section on perception. If you tell a customer that you are Lutheran and every Lutheran they have ever met is a lying shit bag then you yourself are going to be labeled as a lying shit bag.

Part of respecting the beliefs of others is acknowledging their beliefs. To do this you have to consider what the customer is saying and make sure that you don't offend them by not reacting to them. It is important that you take what is said to you and turn it into a positive experience at all times. Keep this in mind when common religious greetings are used as well. One thing I would suggest is that when someone says 'God Bless', respond appropriately. Even if it is out of pure courtesy more than anything else, simply say God Bless or reply, 'to you as well' or 'and you'. Those are appropriate ways to respond without having to accept their 'God' or belief system. If you choose not to respond you risk losing a sale to someone that has the same belief system as the customer. There is a lot of trust when you talk about religion, so to be associated by that person as a member of their community without ever claiming to be, can be a huge part of making a sale to the strongly devout. I know that there are numerous people that would hate the concept of acknowledging religion. Keep in mind, you aren't accepting it as your own, you are simply acknowledging their greeting or statement. To simply ignore it would make you the jackass that just lost a sale.

SPEECH

I don't know why I have to even train people on how to speak. This seems like something that is so incredibly obvious to me. Unfortunately, it appears that it isn't obvious to most of the people that I have trained in the past nor is it obvious to those I run into out in the field. Speech is so incredibly important during a sale that it has to be as close to perfect as humanly possible. Every word that comes out of your mouth is being judged. If you pronounce a word incorrectly, they are going to catch it. If you use a word incorrectly, they'll catch it. If you use improper grammar odds are highly likely that they will catch it. The goal is to recognize what you are doing so that you can prevent yourself from doing it with customers.

When you talk to people, talk like you are intelligent. I don't care who you are talking to, how educated or uneducated they may be, talk as if you are intelligent. If you talk like an idiot, you are going to be perceived as one. Part of being trusted is that you sound like someone that actually has a clue what the hell is going on, even if you really don't. This means that you need to talk using the proper language. Saying things such as "Ain't" or "Aks (as opposed to ask)" is going to make you appear uneducated and probably won't win you any points. I don't give a damn if your momma talks like that, there's no room for it in sales. Sure, you can win some points with your own culture/race when you talk as you normally would, but if they don't know you, then you are going to appear less competent. I guarantee that if you were to go head to head with one of the top sales people in your industry and you started reverting back to your neighborhood slang, you are going to get steamrolled. We all have our slang words but you better forget it during a sales call. You are running the risk of confusing the hell out of the customer.

Being relatively young myself, I understand that language has changed over the years. I realize that many people talk in slang and are educated to the meaning of it due to the modern media. This doesn't mean that you should talk with it during a sales pitch. I don't care if you are talking to someone your own age, talk to them like an adult. There is nothing more annoying than having someone my own age attempt to sell me something. Just because I understand the lingo, doesn't mean that I want to be talked to in that manner. In a professional setting, I want to be shown the respect that I have earned throughout my time on this earth. I want to feel like I am dealing with someone that respects me. When someone begins to talk to me as if I am their best friend from high school, I immediately begin to feel as if I am being talked down to. I am still going to be extremely cordial and talk as he talks, but I am not going to do business with him. The bottom line is that I want to do business with someone I trust not my best friend. Sure, I love my friends, but I don't do business with them either. You aren't trying to make a buddy, you are trying to make money.

The moral of all this is to keep it simple. If you are constantly trying to be like another culture just to get the sale, you are going to fail miserably. People are far more intelligent than we often give them credit for and because of that, they are going to see through what you are attempting to do and it will be looked down upon more often than not. If you are going to talk, you need to do so in a respectful way. Talk to the customer as if they are intelligent, by speaking intelligently yourself. I don't care how old they are, what race they are, or how hip they may appear to be, you should always speak to them with respect using the proper version of the language you are speaking to them in. You can never go wrong by speaking properly, but there is always a chance of going wrong by not. You may think that you are good at morphing into other people, but most of the time you are going to come off as a fake.

CHAPTER 6 :
POUNDING THE
PAVEMENT

am going to assume that you don't have leads dumping in. If you did then you wouldn't need this book or even give a damn about what I have to say. The reality is that everyone in sales at some point in time is going to have to work to generate their leads. This is what makes outside sales different from inside sales. This is what separates us from the car salesperson, the phone salesperson, or the shoe salesperson. We have to actually get out there and work our asses off before we ever even get a chance at making a sale. This of course creates a great deal of issues all its own.

If you never generate the leads then you are going to fail long before you ever get a chance to make a sale. In fact, this is the reason why ALL salespeople that fail will ultimately fail. Think about it, if you are able to generate 10 leads a day and the top salesperson generates 5 you are going to have twice the opportunity. So maybe the top salesperson closes 50% of his leads and you only close 25% you are both still selling 2.5 sales that day. This doesn't mean you'll both make the same amount of money as I imagine the top salesperson will get more for each sale. This does means that if you are good at generating leads you are going to give yourself a HUGE advantage over others in your office. Fortunately for you, most salespeople really suck at this portion of the job and take it too lightly.

For those that work hard at generating more leads on a daily basis they are going to not only have more opportunity but they are going to have more practice. With the practice comes a better lead closure rate which in combination with more leads can mean the ability to jump into the top salesperson bracket. Lead generation isn't as easy as just saying that you are going to do it. There is a lot to it. It takes a lot of work. It means that you have to constantly think about it.

SELF MARKETING

If you are able to market yourself effectively you are going to be able to generate far more leads than you would in any other manner. To better understand the concept that I am attempting to illustrate it is important that you first understand what I mean by the idea of SELF MARKETING. To self market, I truly mean that you are marketing yourself. YOU are the product and service that is being offered. Think of it like a big box of YOURSELF sitting on the shelf for someone to purchase.

Customer A talks to Customer B and tells them that they really enjoy that big box of YOURSELF and that Customer B should give it a try. Customer B may think this over and while they are shopping they see this big box of YOURSELF on the shelf and scoops it up. Sure I could have summarized this by simply saying referrals but this concept goes well beyond a simple referral. When you are self marketing you have to find those that work in a related field that would benefit from having your name on the tip of their tongue. The more people that you have with your name on the tip of your tongue the easier lead generation will be for you. The idea is that you then have people working for you. Unfortunately, this isn't always as easy as we would like it to be, but that's where I can help.

The first step is to identify who you are and what you represent. Assume that you sell pest control services. You need to identify those services that complement what you are already selling. By doing this you are going to now have a list of potential companies or salespeople that you can work with in order to generate leads. If you sell pest control and you have a friend that services pools you may share a similar customer base. These are people that have disposable income that obviously prefer professionals to handle their house maintenance. These people have decided that their time is worth more than the cost of hiring someone to do these services for them. The idea is that rather than working alongside these people in other industries, you work with them. If you find a pool person that you trust make an agreement that you will promote their services when you are with a customer if they do the same. Maybe you can even work out a referral system that allows them to benefit from marketing you. An example of this would be giving $5 for every confirmed inspection that the pool service salesperson sets up for you. This would be additional money for them but could mean substantial new appointments for you. The benefit of this would be that you would now have appointments setup with customers that are more inclined to purchase a SERVICE. This will obviously increase the odds of you selling your service considerably as you are now pitching your service to someone that has the potential of buying from you in the first place.

If you are selling a product you can do the same thing. If you sell pool equipment, you could use the same pool guy as above. The pool guy would simply recommend you whenever a product is required for the pool. Either way, your goal should be to create relationships such as this in order to further develop your lead flow. By having others working for you more leads can be generated than if you were to do it on your own. The great thing about these leads is that they are typically much warmer than those you would generate through cold calling or cold knocking. This means that you SHOULD get a much better response out of them as well.

In order to start the process of having others generate leads for you first you need to create a list of companies/salespeople that could assist you. Assuming that you are still selling pest control you should consider those companies that you see while you are out in the field. These are the other types of companies that are offering services. Again, people that purchase one type of service are going to be far more inclined to purchase another one. I cannot stress enough that these are the types of people that typically consider their time to have a greater value than it would cost to pay someone to render these services for them. So if you sell pest control consider pool services, lawn services, security services, etc. You also need to consider those that provide products and services that overlap what you do in your industry. In the pest control world your major business is probably going to be termite control and treatment. If this is the case then you should work directly with those that are most likely to come in contact with termites and termite damage. You would now create a list of the plumbers, handymen, carpenters, and other home service companies that would be likely to see termite related issues. It is amazing just how many of these people find problems and simply tell the customer that they need to get a termite company to take care of the problem. If you are on the tip of their tongue they are going to tell the customer to call you rather than consulting the phone book. Again, if you give them a referral fee for every lead that they give you they are going to be generating additional income just by doing their job. You could also agree to send them business. If you are at a termite job that needs repair work then you could refer them to your carpenter friend. If the termite problem was made worse by the additional moisture created by a plumbing leak then you could refer your plumbing friend. The idea is that working with others is a lot better than working alone. By doing this you not only get additional leads but you get the benefit of a personal referral which is much stronger than any ad in the yellow pages.

One problem that salespeople run into with this method is that they really don't put effort into it. You aren't typically going to see immediate results with this method. You have to realize that you may only get one referral every couple of months from these sources. This is why you need to have numerous sources. If you average one referral per month from your sources and you have 50 sources you are now generating 50 leads per month without having to put in additional effort towards generating leads. If you consider the amount of time and effort it would take to generate this many leads through cold calling or cold knocking and it can make a huge difference. The idea is that you should always work SMARTER no HARDER.

My recommendation is that you consider breaking down your marketing in a manner that provide the greatest results. Normally I use a 90/10 split. 90% of everything that I do will generate short term results. This would include cold calling, door knocking, generating new sales with current/past customers, winning back customers, mailers, advertising, trade shows, things of this nature. The other 10% of my time I spend working on programs that generate longer term results. While SELF MARKETING is going to create great results in the long term it really doesn't provide much of an instant impact. This is why you really need to take the time to do it but you can't assume it is going to generate instant results either. The reason why you do this conjunction with other programs is simply because these long term results are much more sustainable. When you do a mailer you get an instant hit and it is done. When you advertise on a billboard the same is true. A developed referral network will continually produce leads even if you stopped growing it. The further you develop and grow it the more leads you are going to generate on a regular basis. This is the main reason why salespeople that have been with a company for a long time generate so many leads without working as hard. They developed these referral networks from the beginning and they have continually grown into one that allows them to simply answer their phone all day without having to work to generate leads in the same way that the newer salespeople do. But again, if you work this program too hard in the beginning without also working on those programs that generate shorter term results you are tenure will be short lived.

THE LITTLE BUSINESS CARD THAT COULD

One of the most underutilized forms of marketing is the business card. While most people use it for its original intended purpose sometimes it pays to be a bit more creative. In order to take yourself from being a salesperson to a sales superstar you have to take a little more time to consider the importance of even the most simplistic of tools at your disposal. While you may assume that you are using those tools correctly often times you will find that simply weren't thinking creatively enough.   The idea in this section is that you must consider marketing in everything that you do.

Once you get into a marketing mentality you will find that you can come up with numerous marketing ideas that could ultimately lead to BY CHANCE leads. Typically business cards are used in order to generate AFTER CONTACT sales. This means that you have already made conversation with the contact and you are giving them your card in order for them to contact you in the future. While this is the intended purpose of a business card using it ONLY in this manner means that you are missing out on a great deal of opportunity. This is where the BY CHANCE lead comes in. A BY CHANCE lead is one in which someone picks up your card or information by a CHANCE encounter with it. For example, I go into a flower shop to pick up some flowers but they need a few extra minutes to finish my order. I would normally start looking around the shop to pass the time. Suppose there was a community board in the shop as there are in many shops and restaurants. On this board I might notice the business card for a rental car company. If I was looking for a rental car company this would be incredibly convenient. This could also mean a sale for the person that placed that card. The idea is that while your chances are incredibly low of generating sales through this method every sale that you do generate is a freebie that you wouldn't have gotten if you hadn't placed your card there.

Also, having your name in as many places as possible is important as well. If you were to see a particular business card ten different times in a week you are much more likely to remember that name. Now say you need that service a couple months later you may remember that name and ask for that person when calling the company. While the business card didn't make the immediate sale it could have generate a triggered response when that product/service was needed and ultimately led to a sale. The idea again is that this is a sale that wasn't expected and should be considered a bonus for simply leaving your cards wherever you go.   It is important to do this correctly in order to take full advantage of the opportunities.

CARDS, CARDS, AND MORE CARDS...

Your business card is by far the most economic and useful marketing tool at your disposal. With most employers it doesn't cost you a thing but for some reason they aren't given out nearly enough. The first step for most salespeople is to get into the habit of handing out business cards more frequently. To do this it is important to set a goal. In the beginning I always recommend handing out 5 cards per day but as you get better at it you should work towards handing out 10, 15, or even 20. These cards should be placed in a separate card holder than the ones that you store your normal cards in. This makes it easier to remember that you still have cards to hand out. The hardest part about this is that you can't hand ANY of these cards out to someone that is a current customer of yours. The idea is that you are attempting to generate NEW leads from these cards so they must be in ADDITION to the ones that you would normally handout throughout the day. While handing out five cards seems relatively easy it really isn't. The major issue is that you can't simply give someone a card. It just doesn't work like that. An attempt has to be made to generate conversation with them. This could be something as simple as a conversation at a checkout line. This could be you handing out your card because you stopped to help someone after an accident. It could be giving out your card as opposed to stating it whenever you are required to give out personal information. If you work in commercial sales this tends to be MUCH easier than if you do residential sales. If you work in commercial sales you are going to be a lot of door to door selling which would give much more opportunity to hand out cards. For this reason a commercial salesperson should consider handing out considerably more cards than a residential salesperson would. If you do residential sales and you are running towards the end of the day but you haven't hit your goal try knocking on doors. While this is a somewhat archaic method of getting appointments it is still a somewhat effective one. Just keep in mind that most people work during the day so if you are attempting to knock during the week it could take you a while to hand out all of your cards. However, it is a mentality that we are attempting to change. You have to push to succeed in sales. You have to work towards goals. So to make this work, you have to be willing to work to achieve your goal each and every day.

CARD HANDING TRICKS

By simply handing someone a card doesn't mean that they are ever going to actually look at it. In fact, it is highly likely they will simply misplace it or throw it away altogether. This is why it is a good idea to give them reason to actually inspect the card. By giving them reason to look at the card you are ensuring that they see what you are selling, what company you represent, and hopefully they will remember you for their future needs. One way to do this is to use your card for EVERYTHING. If someone asks you for directions pull out your business card face up and flip it over to jot down directions then hand it to them face up again. This forces them to look at the face of the card before they are able to get to the directions. It also means that they are going to keep the card at least until they get to their destination. Your act of goodwill could also give them more reason to consider you for any future purchase relating to your product/service. This method applies to far more than just directions. Anything that needs to be written down should be done in a similar manner.

Even if the person doesn't appear to be someone that would purchase your product they may drop it in an area where someone that is interested happens to look. Think about it like the seeds of many plants. They require that an animal pick them up in their fur and deposit them in an area that allows them to continue growing into a plant. While not all of the seeds will be successful some will be. The same is very much true with this method of delivery. The idea is simple the more you put your name out there, the greater the opportunity you have for a response. I do have a couple of great tricks that have worked well for me in leaving behind business cards.

- When leaving your card at a restaurant with your tip remember that most of the time the money will be taken and the card left behind for the busser to toss. This is why you should consider making your business card into your tip. To do this, you could fold up the tip and use paper clips to affix it to the card. By doing this, they have to look at your card at least briefly in order to get the tip. They may also be more apt to throw it in their pocket as they are in too much of a hurry to mess with it at that moment. NOTE: If you leave a bad tip, you are only creating negative word of mouth, so only leave your card if you are leaving a proper tip.

- Attach a coin to the back of your cards. By giving the card weight it will immediately feel different than other cards and will draw more attention than if you simply gave your card by itself. This will of course entice the receiver to give your card a look before determining if it is indeed trash.

- Make your card worth keeping. To do this you could place a calendar on the back of your card, you could have a calendar of events, you could make it a magnet with emergency contact numbers, etc. The idea is that you give the person an additional possible reason to hold onto the card. While they may not need the product/service immediately they could very well need it down the road. If this is the case, then having your contact information readily available could be a big deal. This of course is why companies create personalized pens, paper, mini footballs, etc. These types of icebreakers give a company advertising longevity. You should find a way to do the same with even your business card.

ARE YOU A CARD DROPPER?

        Each and every day you probably visit dozens of locations whether you truly realize it or not. Each one of these locations is a viable marketing spot, but unless you are thinking creatively you may have never realized it in the past. What most people never realize or think about is how often you notice simple things that are out of place.

Have you ever noticed a piece of paper floating around a parking lot and looked a little closer? Maybe you have seen an envelope on a countertop and glanced at it. The same is true with most anything in our environment. We are naturally drawn to anything that we subconsciously perceive to be out of place or out of the ordinary. So you should attempt to make yourself and your marketing habits somewhat out of the ordinary. Think of all of the places that you visit throughout the day and start to consider areas that are high visibility that could also be a great place for your own personal billboard: your business card. These placements are your 'BY CHANCE' cards. With each of these placements, you have the opportunity for someone to randomly see your card, realize their own need, and hopefully use it to contact you to fulfill that need.

Throughout each day, an effort should be made to place 10-20 opportunity cards in a variety of locations. Where you place these cards is completely up to you and could become a game to see how creative you can become with their placement. Sometimes the creativity of placement alone could draw the attention of a potential customer. The idea is that with this concept, quantity is king. The more cards that you place the higher the odds will be that someone will contact you.

NOTE: Keep in mind that often times these cards are placed in a purse or wallet to fulfill a future need rather than an immediate one. It is for this reason that results typically come from ongoing efforts rather than in the form of instant gratification.

CARD PLACEMENT IDEAS...

- In the bathroom on the mirror
- Next to a pay phone
- Inside an elevator
- On the checkout stand
- Affixed to your shopping cart
- Inside the menu at a restaurant
- Next to the credit card reader at a gas pump
- In a shoebox at a local store
- On the driver side door of a car parked next to yours
- Inside of a book you picked up at a store

BECOME A PAPER HORDER

It should be your goal to collect every single business card that you come across. I want you to look at business cards as if they are the most sacred treasure in the world and you have the opportunity to seize it. While this may seem like a complete waste of paper, it is in reality, one of the smartest moves you can make. The idea of course is that you have to think outside of the box and if you do so then I'm certain you can come up with numerous ways to find use for these business cards.

The major holdup for most people is that they forget that the person they are taking the card from has a life outside of work. Far too often we look at someone at Wal-Mart and never consider the possibility that they could be a customer, when in reality, they are as likely as anyone else to become a customer. The key is to take every opportunity at your disposal to generate business from each and every contact that you make.

The modern day business card will more often than not include the email address of the person listed on the card. With each card that you collect you are simply adding to your own personal mailing list. If you don't currently have a mailing list, you should consider it as it could be instrumental in generating sales. The key however is to ensure that you are adding the email addresses as you collect them. If you do this, each mailing should only consume as much time as it takes to write the email itself.

In email marketing, you should consider writing these emails during the holidays or special events and on the bottom by your signature, include some sort of promotional offer. The reasoning is that you don't want the email to come across as spam. Far too often people delete email if they don't know who it is from. By eliminating the spam aspect of the email you give the appearance that you are simply wishing well to your contacts. Those reading the email will now look much deeper into the email in an attempt to remember who you are. The goal is that they will dig deep enough to notice the promo in your signature. If this is something they need or will need, they are going to take notice. Just remember that your customer has ever changing needs. While they may not show any interest after the first contact they might after the 5th, 10th, or even the 30th. Persistence is the key to success here.

NOTE: Keep it simple. Keep the text short adding only a few images if desired that don't steal the show from the promo. Remember, the promo is the main part of the email the rest is just a gimmick.

You could also use the addresses on the cards in order to send out greeting cards, mailers, or the like. The more attention you give to this contact, the greater your odds become at doing business with them. Your ultimate objective should be to keep yourself on their mind. By sending out regular emails, mailings, or even text messages you are going to solidify yourself as their premier contact if they or someone they know needs your product in the future.

COLD KNOCKING AND DOOR HANGING

Cold knocking is one of the oldest forms of generating business. It simply consists of walking around a neighborhood and knocking on doors. While this method was very successful when at least one person was typically home in each household it has become a very difficult means of marketing in modern times. For this reason many companies have given up cold knocking in favor of door hanging. Rather than knocking on the doors a crew will go around and hang up door knockers. The idea is that in the amount of time it takes to knock on a door, wait for someone to answer, and communicate with them dozens of doors could have been tagged with door hangers. This method tends to take on the idea that sometimes quantity can trump quality. Personally I feel that there are better uses of your marketing time than door knocking and hanging but it does serve its purpose even today.

Cold knocking and door hanging should be part of your marketing mix it is shouldn't be considered your primary method of marketing as it has a very low rate of return. If you are working during the week, consider door hangers. If you happen to see someone outside or notice that someone is home that is when you should knock and attempt to talk to them. If you don't, just hang up the hanger and move on. Your goal is to use your time wisely to get the most impact for your time as possible. If you are working on the weekend then it may make more sense to try knocking on more doors. People are typically home on the weekends especially early in the day and later at night. Knocking on doors during this time period could result in a much greater rate of success.

While some companies have dedicated entire days to door knocking and hanging I really don't see the utility in this. Sure you could generate a couple of leads here and there but you are taking salespeople out of the field and to me that is self defeating. I recommend instead of killing an entire day to dedicate it to marketing, you simply spend your day more wisely. If you are on a sales call already then you should door knock and hang flyers on 10-15 doors in that general area. By doing this you are going to take full advantage of your time in that area without missing out on a day of sales. If you don't have any sales calls setup for the day then I guess marketing should be done in order to make sure something comes out of the wasted day. The key is that you have to do this on a consistent basis. If you don't hang door flyers every single time you are in a neighborhood then you aren't going to have the impact that you are looking for. The big thing to keep in mind is that you can really only expect a rate of return of about 1 in 100 at best. With low rates of return and a greater amount of effort it is simply better to work smarter rather than harder and do this type of marketing while you are already doing something else.

MAILERS

Probably the most important part of my marketing mix has always been mailers. This is something that you can easily do during your downtime between appointments or while you are watching television at night. The important thing to remember about mailers is that you are probably going to get a response of about 2 out of every 100 depending upon your product/service. It is for this reason that most salespeople give up on mailers altogether.

To make it easier on myself, I try to create a mailing schedule. If I am going to send out a mailer I am going to make certain that I do so in a way that doesn't burn me out. To accomplish this I typically attempt to send out 30 mailers per day. I know that I can easily put together 30 mailers between all of the gaps in my day without stressing myself out. This is a much easier approach to mailers than attempting to do 500 at once. I find that making mailers part of my morning process has made me far more successful than I would have been if I stopped everything to do nothing but mailers. By doing them daily I also create a bit of consistency that makes it a lot easier for setting up appointments as well. The key here is that you have to make sure that you do this every single day. By skipping days you are only reducing the consistency of inbound calls coming directly to you. This is normally where most salespeople fail in direct marketing. If you aren't going to put the effort into it and do it on a regular basis then you aren't going to get the measurable results that you want. It takes a lot of mailers to get even a single phone call and by doing it on a consistent basis you can ensure that you get a regular flow of leads from it.

Technology is another issue with direct mailing. While it has helped to greatly streamline the process it has also made it easier for more companies to send out mailers utilizing very little manpower. This means that the market is far more saturated than it ever was in the past. This of course has drastically reduced the return on mailers over time. If a customer can predict that your mailer is junk mail from a company that they don't currently do business with then they are most likely to throw it out before they ever even look at it. So if you are going to do a mailer you need to attempt to make your mail less predictable. You want a customer to look at it and wonder what is inside of it. To think about it before they simply toss it out. To do this you have to look different that most other junk mail that your potential customer is getting on a daily basis.

What I have found is that when I send out mailers with labels my response rate goes from 2-5 for every 100 to 1-2 for every 200-300. This is substantial difference but I thought about it a little bit more to understand the psychology of it. If I were to get an envelope from a company that I didn't do business with that had a printed label I would assume that it was marketing material and would throw it out without ever opening it. The companies that HAND WRITE the address on the envelope I always seem to open and inspect a bit. This is because I really don't know what is going to be inside. Sure it could be marketing material but often times I wonder why it is hand written and open it to find out rather than simply assuming and tossing it out. It appears that other consumers do the same thing. It may sound ridiculous and it is a whole lot more time consuming but it seems to be effective. Not to mention it is a lot easier to simply hand write your envelopes on a daily basis than it is to worry about getting them printed out. Hand writing gives you greater flexible as to when you can do the mailers and when you cannot. By being able to do them no matter where I am at I find that sometimes I can even do 50-100 in a day just based upon what my schedule looks like.

I always tell my salespeople to look at mailers as a bonus opportunity to make sales. While they may be a bit of work to put together if you are doing it during your downtime then you aren't wasting time at all. Since they are done during time that you typically would sit and do nothing anyway anything that you receive because of them is a bonus. If you look at the sales generated from mailers as extra credit sales then maybe you will be more inclined to continue using this method as it can be very effective if done properly.

It is important to keep in mind that mailers aren't going to fill your schedule. They are meant to make it a little bit easier for you to add appointments during periods of time when you really don't have enough time to do anything else. Unfortunately too many people expect far too much out of a mailer and when they get a small one they simply stop doing it. Consistency is so incredibly important with mailers that the less dedicated ones are the ones that fail at it the quickest.

One thing that may help make your mailing campaign a little more successful is to try adding a penny, a button, or something that sticks out a bit to each of your envelopes. This is something that isn't expected and is really inexpensive. Anything that will allow your envelope to stick out from the others will give your mailer a much greater chance of being seen. Colored envelopes can also make a huge difference if you do it properly. Almost all marketing or billing information seems to come in white envelopes these days. If you really want to draw attention to your envelope try using an unusually colored envelope to draw attention to it. These envelopes will typically cost more than the other ones but if they get a couple more people to take notice they are totally worth it.

STILL POUNDING

While there are numerous other methods of marketing that can be utilized the important thing that I wanted to stress in this chapter was that marketing is about creativity. If you find creative ways to generate business you are going to be far more successful than those that are unable to look outside the box. The most important part is that you stay consistent. If you decide that you are going to knock on 8 doors every time that you go on a sales call then you need to do it EVERY TIME. If you are going to send out 30 mailers per day then you need to do it EVERY DAY. Consistency will not only ensure a regular flow of customers but it will make it easier for you to remember to do it and motivate yourself to do it. Most salespeople that I have trained will typically run these programs for a short period of time but will ultimately fail at it over time because they started getting more and more relaxed when it came to continuing the programs.

To help illustrate the importance of maintaining these programs I will attempt to break it down a bit so that it is a little clearer. Assuming that you work 22 days per month with 5 sales calls on average per day and you stayed consistent with each of the above mentioned programs, here is a simple look at what it could produce for you in terms of leads over a ONE MONTH period of time:

30 Mailers per day (1 in 100 response) – 630 total mailers – 6.3 leads

8 Doors knocked per house, 40 houses a day (1 in 100 response) – 880 total houses – 8.8 leads

10 Business cards dropped per day (1 in 200 response) – 1.1 leads

If you didn't generate any other leads from any other method of marketing then you be generating an extra 16.2 leads per month by simply taking advantage of your free time throughout your work day. If you were to close a typical 1 in 7 of the leads that you run that means you are going to generate an extra 2-3 sales per month. If your average commission is $100-$200 per sale this means an additional $200-$600 per month. Again this is all just extra money that you would gain by simply taking advantage of your downtime. Imagine if you were to double the number of mailers that you do on a daily basis. If you did these things you could considerably increase your income with little additional effort. Even doing these minimal numbers you could make thousands extra per year.

The bottom line to all of this is that you are directly responsible for how much you make. If you are a ground pounder and you are able to work hard and dedicate yourself to selling at least 40-60 hours per week then you are going to find a way to make money. If you find yourself taking constant breaks, talking with your coworkers frequently, or surfing the internet you aren't doing what you need to be doing. This type of dedication is fine when you are getting paid a salary or an hourly wage. This isn't fine when you are depending upon every ounce of effort to pay your bills. You have to be aggressive, you have to take advantage of every minute of the day, and you have to push to make it. If you aren't willing to do this then stop reading this book, stop dreaming of making the big money, and quit. Just quit! You are never going to make it as a salesperson if you aren't willing to put in the time and effort to become one. Just because you have the title, doesn't make you a salesperson. To become a salesperson you have to put in the effort above. You have to be willing to work hard for 40-60 hours a week. You have to be dedicated to making yourself the best in your industry.

CHAPTER 6 :

ASKING QUESTIONS AND CLOSING THE SALE

Throughout this book thus far I have talked about how important it is to be natural when you are selling. To interact with your customers as you would your own family and friends. The same is true with asking the right questions. This doesn't mean that you can ask someone about the massive lump on the side of their neck, why they left piddle on their toilet seat, or why their house smells like dog, it means that you have to ask questions in a manner that shows you actually care about your customer as a person.

For me this section of the book was the absolute hardest. It took me a while to sit down and think about what I do when I am with a customer. What I ask the customer. How I finalize my sales. This is because I never really thought about it before. I just did it. To me this goes to prove that if you are thinking about the types of questions you are asking you aren't doing it naturally.

When I talk to my friends and family I'm not thinking about what questions I need to ask next. I am thinking about their needs, their concerns, and of course attempting to fulfill my own curiosity.

The exact same is true when you talk to a customer for the first time. You are attempting to find out what it is going to take to get them to buy from you. To do this you need to better understand who they are. To do this you are going to ask the customer the same types of questions you would ask someone you know and haven't seen in a while. You are going to probe. As they tell you more you are going to dig a bit deeper. Your goal is to satisfy your curiosity and to stimulate the conversation. This is exactly what you should be doing with each and every one of your customers. You must treat them like any other person in order to take them off of their guard and get them to open up to you and trust you.

I think far too often we are told that we need to have questions prepared in order to discover a customer's needs but if you know how to talk to someone that is going to be relatively automatic with only a few clarifying questions to ensure that you are understanding their needs correctly.

When you are talking to your friends and family you would use similar questions as you should use with your customers. You wouldn't ask your friends and family simple yes/no questions (close ended) so why would you ask your customers these types of questions? Think about how you speak to those around you and you'll quickly realize that you push for conversation with those that you care about so you ask them questions that are going to strike up a conversation. The same is true with your customer. These open ended questions are going to open up the other person and obviously you are going to obtain more information from them in the process.

For example:

Is Vermont nice? (close ended)
- This type of question wouldn't be asked to a family member so it shouldn't be the type of question that you ask a customer. It simply shows the person that you are talking to that you are only interested in a short response. They may give you this "yes" or "no" response and move on. By asking this type of question you are eliminating the

possibility of receiving more voluntary information that an open ended question would draw out.

What is it like living in Vermont?

- In this type of question you would get far more information than "yes" or "no" because that would be an improper response to the question. In this you may get a simple response but odds are more likely that they are going to give much more detail in the response. They could tell you that they love going to the markets on Sunday. From this information you are now able to assume that the customer enjoys going to the market on Sunday.

While this may not seem to be important information it can help you to see what type of a person you are talking to. It can also help to establish reason why this person may or may not do something.

If a customer were to tell you that they love the churches in Vermont you could conclude that you are talking to someone that is religious. This of course can direct how you communicate with the customer. It will also help you determine what they would and would not be interested in. If you are selling gift items door to door and you now know that they belong to a church that doesn't practice Halloween you can use this information to eliminate any part of your pitch that may include Halloween gift ideas.

Not only will these bits of information potentially save you from making stupid mistakes that you may regret later they can help guide you into asking further questions or pushing the conversation further.

One thing that I have always found is that the more the customer talks the more likely they are to give you the business. This isn't because people that talk are easier to sell. This is because people that talk are displaying trust. If someone doesn't trust you they aren't going to give you information especially information of a personal nature. It is important though that you listen in a situation like this so that you can respond to what they are saying. The more attentive you are the more likely you are to gain their business. People want to do business with someone that they like and trust. This is why your friends and family are going to be more likely to buy from you. They are going to trust you more than they are going to trust some random salesperson. The same is going to be true with someone that you get to open up.

The important thing to realize is that most customers are only going to supply you with information if you seem to be interested in what they have to say. If the customer has a garden ask them what types of things they grow in the garden. If the customer has a lot of pictures all over their wall ask them how big their family is. By asking these types of questions you are feeding their sense of self.

People love to talk about their accomplishments, their families, and everything that has to do with them. Your job is to ask the right questions to allow them to do this. During the process you should attempt to talk as little as possible and listen as much as possible. The more you talk the greater chance you have of ruining the sale. The more they talk the greater chance you have of obtaining the sale. During the questions you can easily ask them about their needs for your products and services. By mixing between "friendly" questions and product questions you are giving the customer a comfortable environment to communicate.

Here is an example conversation that would be effective at both creating general conversation and trust while still building the sale. In this scenario assume that I am selling pest control services.

Myself : *While inspecting your home I noticed some termite damage inside your incredible collectibles room. How long did it take you to collect all of those action figures?*

Customer : *I have been collecting since I was a child. I find a few new items a month and have kept it going. It is something that I really enjoy doing to release stress and it something I hope I can pass on to my two boys when they get older.*

Myself : *I imagine with something so important you I am certain you want to protect it then, right?*

Customer : *I have spent a great deal of time on this collection and it would horrible if I lost it.*

Myself : *I'm sure your sons would love to continue this passion. I can tell that you really enjoy it so I want to make sure that I assist you in taking care of it. When would be a good day for you to resolve the problem?*

Alright, there are a lot of things that happened in this round of conversation. Every bit of the conversation while natural had some built in intent. I told the customer first about the damage that I discovered in order to observe their initial reaction. Anyone that has a large action figure collection probably cares a great deal about it. By watching their reaction I could tell just how important it would be for them to protect this collection. This will help me in determining the price. If I get little to no reaction I am going to keep the price more affordable. If I notice a major reaction then I am going to price it higher with more specialty services to ensure COMPLETE PROTECTION for this customer.

The next thing that I want you to notice is that I followed my statement with a question about their collection. I wanted to first show the customer interest. By showing customer that you are interested in who they are you are giving them permission to open up and talk about everything that makes them who they are. The question itself was open ended so it forced the customer to respond with more information than a simple "yes" or "no".

The customer during his response gives me information that I can use throughout the rest of the selling process. Notice that the customer states that they have been working on this collection since they were young. This is important because this tells you that the customer is dedicated to this collection. This is their life work. If they balk at the treatment you can restate that this is something they have worked their entire life on and it would be a shame to see it destroyed by termites when it could be resolved so easily and inexpensively. The customer also volunteered information about his family. You now know that the customer has two boys that are younger. He is obviously interested in sharing this collection with them so the collection has obvious sentimental value to him.

My response is what is called a TIE DOWN. A Tie Down is where you relate to a customer while asking them a question that cannot generate a "no" answer. By first stating that the collection is obviously important I am assuming that the customer agrees with me. By asking the question "right?" I am simply training the customer to start saying "yes". The more a customer says "yes" the harder it is going to be for them to say "no" when it comes time to close the sale. During this question I would also nod my head up and down to encourage the "yes" response.

What the customer says next is a typical response that someone would say to a TIE DOWN. Like I said before, the TIE DOWN is meant to tie the customer down. Think of it like the stakes when putting up a tent. Sure the rods are important but if you don't have something to hold the tent down it is going to get blown around. The same is true with a customer. If the customer isn't tied down you are going to open up the possibility for both "yes" and "no" responses at random. In other words much like your tent, your customer is going to be tossed around until they reach a final position. Your goal is to tie them down early in the process to assist them in making that decision from the beginning.

My next response shows that I care about what the customer has said. I show that I have been listening to the customer in regards to his wishes for his collection. I also show that I care about the customer and his passion for collecting. I show that I want to protect it and of course take care of the customer in the process. I am assisting him with his problem, not selling him on one. I then assume the sale by stating, "I can tell that you really enjoy it so I want to make sure that I assist you in taking care of it. When would be a good day for you to resolve the problem?" This is a trial close. If the customer gives me a date, then I start the paperwork and finish the sale. Most likely the customer is going to balk as this attempt to close with questions about price, about what the treatment involves, etc. My goal isn't to kill him with details until details are necessary to close him.

Far too often I find salespeople attempting to beat the customer with details. While these details are going to be important to some they aren't going to be important to the majority. Keep in mind that the more you talk the more likely you are to create more questions and potentially lose the sale. You are the one that is doing the questioning. You are the one that is controlling the sale. If you are asking the correct questions while at the same time creating conversation with your customer they are going to be much less resistant to doing business with you.

The main reason why I have always added personal details into the conversation with a customer is to create a distraction. When you are talking to a customer about business and business alone they have their game face on. They are waiting for you to attempt to close the deal. They are waiting to use their rebuttals that they already have prepared. By creating conversation you are generating a distraction that will allow you to sneak in a trial close that they may not be ready for. If they aren't ready for it they may simply allow the sale to happen. If they don't they are probably going to throw out a "real" objection as opposed to a polished one.

"Real" objections can be overcome with extra information or conversation. "Fake" objections cannot be overcome as they are "Fake". If you attempt to overcome a "fake" objection you aren't going to resolve the "real" ones and you aren't going to resolve the issues that are stopping the customer from buying your product/service.

It takes time and confidence to create perfect conversation. If you are already smooth at talking to people then this is going to be a lot easier. If you struggle and stutter a lot during conversation it is going to be incredibly difficult to smoothly distract a customer in this manner.

Another reason for adding personal details into a conversation is because it allows your customer to relate to you as a person, not as a salesperson. I always told my salespeople that if a customer were to ever call the office and ask to talk to Richard the Salesperson I wasn't doing my job. My job was to SELL them on the concept of me being there to ASSIST them in resolving their problems whether they knew they had one or not prior to my visit. If you do pest/termite control this means that you are an inspector. If you do magazine sales you are a print consultant. I don't care what the hell you call yourself as long as you realize it is about YOU helping the CUSTOMER make a decision. The sooner you realize you are HELPING and not TELLING the better you will be at SELLING your customer.

By asking the proper questions you are going to be able to find out what the customer's needs are and you are going to HELP resolve those needs. Sure the customer may not have had a clue that they had a termite problem prior to my visit in the example above but I was able to HELP him to resolve that problem. I took personal interest in the protection of his valuables and as such I probably would have closed the sale.

GETTING THE BUSINESS

Getting to the business can be frustrating for most salespeople because they think that they are so close. In most situations I find that it really could have been a couple of words that prevented someone from closing out a sale the same day. The biggest problem is that the salesperson is afraid to ask for the business. The other problem is that far too often a salesperson will avoid asking for the business by trying to build up the product so much that they feel the customer has no choice but to buy. The problem is that this isn't going to ACTUALLY make them buy. This is going to create more questions and a whole hell of a lot more confusion. When you are trying to get the business you need to only tell the customer what they need to know in order to get them to buy. Every detail above and beyond this is a detail that could destroy the deal completely.

To make it a little bit easier for those of you that are technical geek bags I have decided it would be worthwhile to break the customer thought process down for you. It involves four basic questions so brace yourself:

1. **What is my need/problem?**
   Why do they need what you are offering? What problem do they Have?

2. **What the hell can you do to resolve it?**
   Why is your product/service the one they should use to resolve their issue?

3. **How much does it cost?**
   How much are they going to have to hand over to you in order to make this solution happen?

4. **When can you start?**
   Holy crap everything in their world is going to hell and they need a resolution and FAST.

I know that these four questions seem incredibly simple but they show the actual needs of your customer during your interaction. They don't care about the super duper monster suction of your vacuum. They don't want to know that your knives were polished 2 billion times by mechanically engineered hamsters. They really don't give a shit about your uncle who founded the company by selling painted rocks to children that didn't know any better.

When you start answering other questions that they never asked for answers to you start telling them that their questions weren't good enough. When you do this you are simply telling the customer that they aren't prepared enough to make a buying decision today because there is so much more that they need to know. So for the love of everything SALES please just answer the four questions and shut the hell up! Shut up! Shut up! Shut up! Shut.... UP!

Now that we have established that screwing up a sale is incredibly easy when you over utilize your face hole maybe we can focus on actually getting the business.

If you actually took the time to read the introduction to the book then you realize that I really don't give a shit about what any other salesperson has said about closing out a sale. Sure I may use a lot of similar methods but that's because I didn't create anything new. All I have done with this book is focus on the shit that really matters. I'm not going to go over all of the details to getting the sale. I am not going to go over numerous methods of closing the sale. I am simply going to talk about what works and what works well.

The first thing that you need to realize about getting the business is that you aren't going to sell shit if you aren't confident about it. If you say things like, "and what not", "or something", or my favorite "you know what I am saying" then you are going to sound like you are nervous. If you sound nervous the customer is going to assume that you either don't know what the hell is going on or you are hiding something. I know I wouldn't buy from a customer that I felt was full of shit or something that I felt was a snake. So before you ever attempt to close the sale make sure that you are speaking with confidence. If you do that closing out the sale is going to be MUCH easier.

Next thing that you are going to want to do is focus on assumption. To some people this makes them feel like they are being too arrogant but sometimes that is part of being a successful salesperson. By assuming the sale you are showing the customer that you are ready to do business with them. You are showing them that you are serious about this and you are making them feel as if NOT doing business with you would be out of the norm.

The process of assumption needs to begin with the very first handshake. You need to start talking about the sale from the first words that come out of your mouth. This means greeting your customer with something along the lines of "lets see what's going on so that I can create a plan to resolve it". You would first introduce yourself and all of that but the idea is that very early in the conversation you need to establish that you intend on doing business with this person. By telling the customer that I am going to create a plan to resolve the issue I am telling them that I plan on being the one to resolve it. If you start by telling the customer that you are there to give them a quote you are telling them that you plan on leaving them to make a decision. This means that you are assuming you ARE NOT going to make the sale.

With every aspect of your sale you need to use assumptive words and phrases. If you are talking to a customer about your super awesome knives then you need to tell the customer during your demonstration that THEY WILL LOVE CUTTING

WITH THESE KNIVES. By saying things like this you are giving them ownership of the idea of having these knives. You are starting the process of them thinking about chopping up things with the knives. Most importantly you are again showing them that you expect them to purchase these knives and doing otherwise would be incredibly unusual.

When you close the sale you need to keep on assuming that they are going to purchase whatever it is you are selling. If you are selling alarm systems for their home ask them if Wednesday would be a good day to get their system installed. Ask them if they would prefer a morning or evening installation. The idea is to show the customer that you are so confident in what you are selling and your pitch that you believe they are going to buy it from you. Sure they could still object to your assumptive close but there are a lot of people that will simply let you close them this way rather than attempting to fight it out. Sometimes it is just easier for them to agree to being closed than to deal with another presentation from another salesperson.

One thing to keep in mind with every attempt to close the sale is that once you make a closing statement you need to shut your mouth.

Typically in a situation where you are closing the sale the first person to talk is going to lose. If you force the customer to talk first they are going to either throw out an objection or accept the sale outright. Either way you are going to control the direction of the sale. If you are the first one to speak you are going to buy them more time to come up with an objection or possibly talk them out of the sale altogether.

I cannot stress enough that when you are closing, even trial closing, you need to stay confident and by doing so SHUT YOUR MOUTH. Ask for the business and stop talking. That awkward silence is the best friend that a salesperson could possibly have. The moment you violate it is the moment you sabotage your own sale. Don't be a saboteur, be smart, make the sale.

THE FINAL APPEAL

Take note that I went over assumptive selling and nothing else. This is because salespeople tend to focus so much on all the other bullshit in between that they lose sight of how simple it is to make a sale. You just need to answer the four questions that I talked about earlier and you are well on your way to making the sale. If you didn't answer those four questions properly then the customer isn't going to feel the need to buy your product, they may not understand their problem or why it is such a big deal, or they may simply balk at your price. If you gave them enough information to satisfy them and you offer a product that they actually want then they are going to buy from you. You just have to remember to be confident enough to assume the sale.

I do have just one more trick that I think is important as part of the selling process. While I truly believe in the assumptive sale there are times when assumptive selling isn't enough. This is typically because you messed up somewhere in the sales process. It is impossible to be perfect every single time you talk to a customer but there is a way to bring the sale back under your control if you find that you lost it.

Your last ditch effort as you are packing up everything and getting ready to leave your sale is to be direct with your customer. Tell your customer that you take your job very seriously and because of that you feel like if you don't make a sale you should at least learn something from it. Then simply ask the customer what you could have done differently or what you could have explained better to have made the sale the same day. By this point in time the customer is thinking the sales process is already over with and they are going to feel more open to tell you more. More often than not they are going to tell you what their objections were which will give you one more shot to overcome their objections and ask for the sale one last time. This is your final effort and often times you can walk away with the sale by simply asking this question.

What I want you to realize is that just because it appears you have lost the sale doesn't mean that all is lost. A sale is only lost when you stop trying. This doesn't mean the moment that you leave the customer. This means the moment that you stop attempting to sell the customer. This means that you stop calling them, you stop emailing, you stop sending cards, you simply stop making contact with them altogether. This is when you have lost the sale. Until you give up completely you should always consider what options you have and attempt to use those options to your advantage.

HANDLING OBJECTIONS

Objections are inevitable in sales. You are going to run into them each and every day but you have to become a master at overcoming them so that you can close out the sale. The better that you are at dealing with them the more successful you are going to be overall. The problem is that each customer is going to have a different reason for objecting so it is important that you learn with every customer which methods work and which ones don't.

While I could go over the thousands of different objections a customer could possibly throw at you I really don't think that is going to serve any real purpose. The reasoning is relatively simple, memorization will make you sound scripted. The more scripted you sound the more you become a robotic salesperson. In my opinion this is the best way to kiss a sale goodbye. So rather than attempting to make you a textbook perfect salesperson I am going to ATTEMPT to educate you without doing too much and ruining you.

An objection can be a couple of things. It could mean that the customer simply doesn't understand enough to make a final decision. It could mean that the customer doesn't have the ability to use or afford the product. It could mean that the customer isn't hearing anything positive enough to make them purchase today.

As a salesperson you need to focus on figuring out what the true objection is. If the customer is telling you that they simply can't afford it and you don't have payment options then there is a good chance that they legitimately can't afford it. To resolve this you could simply ask them what they could afford to do. When you ask them this you force them to place a value on what you are offering. Once they place a value on it you can then get approval to meet that price, you could find a different product/service that could meet their needs at a lower price, or you could realize that you simply can't help this customer.

If the customer is telling you that they need to consult with their spouse before they make a final decision they may very well need to speak with their spouse. To find out if this is the case you can ask them whether or not they believe their spouse would be interested in what you are offering or ask them what aspects of what you are offering would interest them. If you can get them talking sometimes you can give them a trial close by saying simply saying one of the following:

1. *It sounds like you know your husband/wife very well and that they would trust your judgment in doing this today.*

This is assuming that sale even though the customer just told you that they don't want to do it. If the

---

customer stops you again they are going to give you a more legitimate objection.

2. *I am going to go ahead and fill out the paperwork, I'm sure your spouse will trust your judgment but if not you have three days to change your mind.*

While this may not sound like a solid close it really is. Most people aren't going to call and cancel a sale once they have already accepted it. This requires effort and fortunately we are a lazy people. Your goal is to leave the house with a commitment and that contract is your commitment that they are going to do business with you. They may change their mind later but that gives you another opportunity to close them again this time you'll have a real objection to counter.

The only other real objection that is tough to counter in the field is the competition objection. The customer may tell you that they would like to obtain other quotes. To counter this you could do numerous things but the easiest is to guarantee your price. If you have price flexibility then you could tell the customer that if they are able to obtain a written quote from a similar company using a similar product then you would be willing to match their price. This can be a difficult one to accomplish so a lot of times it is safer to try other methods of countering on this one.

I personally like to remind the customer about the amount of time they spent working with me. I ask them if they really want to deal with another company coming through and talking to them forever when they could be starting the service or using their product. Often times by reminding them of the hassle of speaking to a salesperson they will simply do business with you to avoid having to deal with it.

Another way to overcome the competition objection is to ask the customer what it would take to get their business today. One of my favorite ways to do this is to counter with:

"By saying that you would like to have other quotes you are telling me that you have a set price in mind that I haven't hit. Tell me that price and I will do what I can to accommodate your needs and save you the hassle of having numerous companies take up more of your valuable time."

This goes right back to showing the customer that you value them as a person. You care about their time and you care about their needs. By showing them that you are going to make an effort to hit their price and meet their needs as a consumer you are reassuring them that you are the right company to do business with.

There are tons of objections that customers will use on a regular basis. My goal isn't to try to teach you how to overcome each and every one of them. This is something that you will learn with time and practice. Most of the objections are going to have simple counters. Some of the questions are going to be a bit more difficult and seemingly impossible to overcome. The idea is that you stay confident in what you are selling and that you continue to control the flow of the conversation and that you keep everything positive. If all else fails use the Last Chance close and see if you can pull them back in.

CHAPTER 7 :
NOT YOUR
AVERAGE CRAP
BAG

Competition can be one of the most challenging aspects of selling. The customer may desire what you are offering but if the competition presents it in a manner that is more appealing you probably aren't going to get that sale. By knowing what you are doing each time you go up against competition you are going to have a much easier time winning the battles and over time will grow to love competing for each and every sale.

For the experienced salesperson there is nothing more rewarding than winning a competitive battle. When there are two equally matched companies with similar products and both salespeople are equally qualified it can be a great feeling to win the battle. Sometimes just winning one of these competitive duals can generate enough confidence that you will increase your closing rate considerably for quite some time.

Before you are able to win in competition you really have to know what it takes to win. The more than you know about what the customer is looking for and what your competition is going to do the better chance you have of beating out the competition . A sale with competition is much different than one where you are only competing with yourself. The biggest reason for this is that you already know that by having competition the customer is serious about buying your product/service. By knowing this you can already rule out the lack of need or necessity as an objection to not buying from you.

The best way to handle objections throughout the process when dealing with competition is to know your competitors better than they know you. This can be somewhat difficult if you don't know who you are going up against. This is why it is so important to be prepared ahead of time. Before you ever step foot in a customer's door you should have shopped your competition and should have a good feel for what you are going up against. For me this meant calling up my competition and having them come and pitch me. This would not only allow me to see what they have to offer but it would give me a good opportunity to get copies of all of their contracts. These contacts would then give me something to study so that I could know the ins and outs of everything that they offer. If I can explain all of the details on every competitor contract without hesitation the customer is going to quickly realize just how well I know the industry that I am in.

Knowing your competition can also give you a huge advantage in countering objections that are related to competition. One thing that I have always done to make this job much easier is create a binder that has contracts with the contract flaws highlighted. If a contract states something that is less than what your contract offers you need to highlight it. DO NOT highlight anything that is better than your contract because this is going to be self defeating. If your contract says the same thing you probably don't want to highlight it because you don't want to draw attention to negatives in your own contract.

It is important to realize though that if you are going to bring out contracts and talk about the competition the customer is going to want to hear about yours. This of course will only be of benefit if your contract is better than your competitors.

Regardless of how your contract stacks up it is a good idea to know your competition and their offerings as well as you know your own. This knowledge will assist you in pushing different products or services that would allow your proposal to be more appealing. A good example of this would be if you are selling vacuums and you are going up against a competitor that has a top level vacuum that you can't compete with. By knowing this you can push the mid level vacuum as being more than enough to handle the needs of the customer and make it appear to be a waste to have that top level vacuum. By doing this you are going to give the customer reason to assume that your competitor only pitched the high vacuum because they want to make money not because they are attempting to give the customer the best vacuum to fit their individual needs. If you didn't have this knowledge then you would have pitched your highest vacuum in a manner that would have allowed the competition to blow you away. You have to give your apple the best opportunity to compete against the competitor's apple.

BUILDING YOUR KNOWLEDGE

Assume that you work in the pest control industry. You had your competition come out and do an inspection on your home for termites. Each of the competitor's talks about what their company will do to treat for termites. They may have different products that they use, they have different methods, but assume that they are all using the same product/method. Now, take a look at their contract.

What does their protection cover?
- Do they cover repair of damages by termites?
- Do they have a limit to how much damage they cover?
- Do you have to pay a deductible?
- Do you have to pay an annual renewal to keep it going?
- Is it required that you retreat and pay the cost of treatment every so many years?

These are just a few things that you could look for in a contract. However, you could also figure out if the competition is even licensed or insured. This of course is very important if you are selling home improvement products. If the contractor was to do substantial damage to a home, then the homeowner could be on the hook for it, if the contractor bails on them.

By knowing what your competitor's contract says you are able to then hype the benefits of your own as compared to the competition.

What you need to realize is that just like everything else in sales you have to be committed to it. The more dedicated you are to the craft, the more sales you are going to generate. It is important that you know your competition. If you don't know how they operate, know their contracts, know their policies, their products, or even their background and history you could set yourself up for failure. There is nothing worse than having a customer ask you a question that you should know the answer to. By not knowing this answer it could potentially mean the difference between closing the deal or not. A customer's only objection may be that they don't know the difference between your company and your competition. By having that information in print available to them you can quickly point out the positives for your company and highlight the negatives of theirs.

IMPORTANT NOTE : You should NEVER bad mouth your competition. Highlight facts only. If you are able to provide proof of the negatives of doing with your competition it is going to look MUCH better than you simply stating a bunch of facts. As a consumer myself there is nothing that I hate more than hearing about how shitty another company is. Facts in print are going to be far more effective than anything that comes out of your mouth in this scenario. The bottom line remains the same, you have to know your competition and take the time to gather information about them.

When you have competition ahead of you prepare yourself extensively. The more you know about them the easier it will be for you to prepare your presentation accordingly.

Things to ask yourself when facing competition
- *Who has the better product/service?*
- *Who has the better brand?*
- *Who has the better price?*
- *Who has the better presentation?*
- *Who has the better contract?*

Hopefully you are working for the largest company in the industry when you face competition, with the best product/service, and the best price. If you are, then you shouldn't have any excuses for not making the sale. However, if you are one of the majority that aren't working for the best of the best, then you really need to plan your approach carefully. This doesn't mean that you have to script every word of your presentation it means that you simply have to know enough to be able to counter even the best salespeople from even the largest of companies.

KNOWING THE COMPETITION

As mentioned before one of the most effective means of learning about your competition is to allow them to sell to you. This is great for numerous reasons beyond just gaining the contracts. You can even use this to hear a variety of different sales pitches that may even make you a better salesperson. The idea is that you take something from every sales pitch that you hear.

If you hear something that you like you can then take that and add it to your own pitch. Your goal should be to bring something positive out of each encounter that could potentially help you sell more effectively.

This is far more effective than even watching role plays in your office. During role plays you miss out on the natural selling instinct and get the scripted company approved method. While this is great for practice it keeps those that are watching from learning a lot of the things that it takes to be really successful.

By watching others do it naturally you are going to get a much better feel for what it takes to be successful. You'll notice what you don't like about their pitch and know what not to do. You'll see things that you like that you'll then be able to use yourself. You should also learn quite a bit about the other company in the process. It can be quite the learning experience if you do it correctly.

STORY FROM THE FIELD

There was a time when I was going up against two salespeople that I had gone up against several times. I knew them to be two of the best in the industry and definitely the best in their respective offices. I knew that they were not only going to be aggressive in their pricing, but they were going to attempt to sell it before I ever got a chance to give my pitch. I knew that not only would I need to disrupt the momentum of my competition in their sales pitch but that I would have to give a better pitch in general. These salespeople are the best of the best and I knew that if I could beat them out for the sale that I was truly as good as I thought I was.

The first stage was to run distraction. I wasn't attempting to distract the competition, I was attempting to distract the customer. The first step was to call the customer and let them know that I had arrived. By doing so I gave them the opportunity to tell me how to proceed. If the customer wanted me to get started with my inspection while the competition was there, then great. If the customer wanted me to wait until they were gone, at least I knew they would give me a shot to pitch because I was already there. In this instance, the customer asked me to begin my inspection while they finished up with the other guy.

I was the second one to give the pitch so I knew that I was going to have to make an impressive showing. As my competitor went around with the customer, I walked around the house as well. I never walked with the two of them but I did walk close enough that the customer was constantly looking back at me. The idea was to stay just off the corner of their eye the entire time so that they were always aware that I was there doing something. This caused the customer to glance over at me on numerous occasions as they saw me do something that they didn't see the other inspector do. I started measuring things that I would typically never measure. I started poking at things that I normally wouldn't poke at. The idea was to look much more thorough than the inspector ahead of me. If I could do this then I could appear as if I was more knowledgeable and willing to go the extra mile to ensure the customer received the best possible inspection and of course the best possible service.

The salesperson knew what I was doing and decided to move the conversation inside. I was hoping that they would keep it outdoors and start talking about pricing in front of me. However, with experience you learn that this is the absolute worst idea and because of that he did the right thing and took the customer inside to sit at the table. While they were inside I knew that I needed to again break up that momentum. To do this I started pulling tools out of my car and tossing them on the road. While I typically only use a couple of tools the additional noise made the customer wonder what could possibly be going on outdoors. They didn't hear this when the other inspector was inspecting so what was I doing that was so different. The key to keep in mind is that while you may not be doing anything more than your competition it is important to give the appearance that you are.

After the door opened and my competitor walked out, he looked over at me shaking his head. I knew that I had accomplished my goal. I now had to do everything that I saw the inspector do but more thoroughly. I had to take the time so that I could discredit the inspection of my competition. As I went along, I would describe everything that is going on around the house. By doing this I was not only able to ask the customer more questions, I was also able to prove to the customer that I had great knowledge of what was happening around their house. Rather than walking them around the house, I walked the customer everywhere. We went around that ¾ acre lot inspecting it if we were looking for buried treasures on the beach with a metal detector.

The next step was to take the time to tell the customer about other issues or concerns that they had in their home. This included inspecting their attic insulation levels, inspecting their water heater, and checking out numerous other areas and making recommendations on those as well. I wanted to prove to this customer that I truly cared about what was happening inside of his house. I didn't want him to think that I was simply there to make a sale. I wanted him to believe I was there to assist him in protecting his home in general.

I remember even going as far as climbing onto the roof of the house. Sure it was scary and I didn't have a clue what I was looking at but the customer seemed to be very impressed by this. Luckily, I was even able to find a hole in the roof that was created by a fallen branch. This of course led to a closer inspection which discovered a great deal of water damage inside of the house. So by doing this I was even able to assist the customer in discovering a problem before it became even worse. Doing things like this shows the customer that I really do care. I wanted to show him that I would help him above and beyond simply what made me money.

By the time I was done with the inspection, I had already given the customer the entire pitch. They had already spent a great deal of time walking around with me and asking me questions so I know that they knew exactly what the issues were and what we were going to do in order to resolve them. Since I knew that I gave a better presentation than the previous inspector and the customer still hadn't heard the presentation of the third I had two real options. I could simply give the customer my contact information and the quote and leave which is what most salespeople would do or I could close it out. I decided that I was going to go for a hard close and finish off the process.

Looking dead at the customer I said to him, "I am sure you can agree I provided you with the highest quality inspection which is reflection on our dedication to the customer experience. I would love to provide your services and save you another hour or two waiting for another inspector. In order to do this I am going to need to know what you are looking to pay for this level of service. By giving me a price you are going to get the service you want at the price you want allowing you to make a decision without further delay". After doing this, I shut my big fat face flap. By talking I would potentially ruin the sale by keeping my mouth shut I would force him to either give me another objection or to actually give me the price that he needs to be at. Once he gives me that price, I know that he sees me as the person he wants to do business with and it is just a matter of doing paperwork from there. In this example I assumed the customer was going to do business with me as long as I hit his price point. I assumed that I did everything else better than my competition and because of that just had to overcome the price objection and I would have the sale. While this can be a somewhat direct method of closing out the sale it can be incredibly effective if you are able to shut your mouth and wait for the customer to react to it. Unfortunately far too many salespeople keep running their mouth while the customer is thinking. This shows a lack of confidence and prevents that awkward silence that forces them to talk. This method works especially well with people that are very social in nature. That dead silence can be a death blow to them and they want to start up the conversation again as quickly as possible.

This method can be used on most sales even if you don't have competition that you are going against. However if you do have competition it can really only be used in this exact manner If you know that you offer a similar product, that you did a better presentation, and that your customer is definitely going to buy. This is going to force out the price objection which is probably the most common of objections and allow you to close out the deal. If you are able to overcome pricing from the start then you not only control the conversation but you eliminate the major reasoning for a customer not doing business with you.

When the customer finally broke the silence he me that he appreciated how thorough I was and said that he was looking to be in a particular price range. I met his pricing needs and we closed out the business. This of course isn't always possible in some areas of sales because you don't have that type of price elasticity. However, if you are in an industry with a great deal of price elasticity then you should always be able to overcome the most serious of objections, which is the price objection by simply asking the customer what they are looking to pay. For some reason I never see anyone else use this method, but it can be extremely effective in closing out a sale quickly. Another method would be to simply ask, "What would keep you from doing business with me today?" Both of these questions are going to generate similar types of responses. The idea is that you are going to get the customer to tell you what all of their objections are so that you can overcome each one and get the sale.

This example shows that by knowing my competition, I knew that I had to go above and beyond for this customer. I did things that I would never think about doing on a daily basis, but I did so to prove that I was going to do whatever it took to make that sale. One thing to keep in mind is that most people want to get the bidding process over with. There is nothing fun about sitting around all day and taking bids. If you are able to give them quality from the start they are going to trust what you have to say. If you are then able to meet their pricing needs they have absolutely no reason to not do business with you. It is important that you realize this and take advantage of it. You are doing the customer a favor by giving them the best product at the best possible price. It is important that you take full advantage of this when closing out the sale. You do have to keep in mind however that if you were the first inspector and you didn't do the best possible job you could have you probably aren't going to be able to grab that sale immediately. It is up to you to be the best and prove to the customer that you are the best without having to say it.

CHAPTER 8 :
MILKING THE COW

$\mathcal{A}$s you begin to grow your customer base you are going to realize that referrals are getting much easier to come by. You are going to have more people sending you business than you ever did in the beginning. You are going to find that you don't have to work quite as hard on each sale. Things are going to get considerably better. Unfortunately, most of this doesn't happen until after you have been doing it for quite some time.

One thing that you have probably already noticed is that there is an overabundance of salespeople that have been selling whatever the hell it is you sell for a year or less. The reason for this is typically burnout. When you are in sales if you aren't constantly working your customer base you are going to put a lot of man hours in attempting to maintain or grow your income. You are going to put a lot of strain on your relationships, your family, and of course your own body. Those that learn to work smarter are the ones that are ultimately going to become the next generation of seasoned sales professionals that stick with the company for years.

Working your customer base is incredibly important in the beginning of your career as that is what will ultimately support you throughout the years. It will keep you from getting burned out attempting to generate all of those leads on your own. It is what will help keep you fierce and will give you the freedom that the other salespeople don't have. With this said, you can't be a piece of shit. You have to work. Let me repeat this and read it carefully. **YOU CANNOT BE A PIECE OF SHIT AND EXPECT TO GET AHEAD LONG TERM**! I am certain that this isn't going to make sense unless I break it down into more simplistic terms that even my young son would understand and appreciate.

Food that is released from the body is no longer useful to the body. It is unable to provide nutrients so the body sees it as waste and eventually releases it. So if you are a piece of shit within your company that means that you have been with the company for a while and your ability to contribute is continuing to lessen. Once you no longer provide any real value to the company you are removed from the company. In a sense, the company shits you out. Sales shits you out! While this may be a horribly crude and disgusting analogy for the life cycle of a salesperson it is reality. Salespeople don't turn into butterflies they either turn into a feeding tube or they get flushed. It is up to you to determine your value. You can either keep feeding the company and thus your family or you can be shit out and forgotten much like a piece of shit.

Just because you have been with a company and working in sales for years doesn't mean that the leads are just going to come your way. Even with time you have to put in effort in order to maintain your referral base. You have to make sure that you are constantly "milking the cow" to ensure that you are getting the most out of it. You have to constantly ask yourself if you are 'useful' to the company. The moment you stop working your customers and growing your referral base is the moment you start sliding out of your company en route to becoming a long forgotten piece of shit.

As you can tell I take this section of the book very seriously. I cannot stress how important it is to your career that you work your base. You worked hard to develop that base you can at least work a fraction as hard to maintain it. It is far easier to maintain current customers than it is to find new ones. Just keep in mind that this process takes some time. If you put in the effort and you give it a chance it will provide you with years of rewards.

Most salespeople don't make it long term for two major reasons:
     1. They never put in the effort in the first place.
     2. They don't give it enough time.

I think it is obvious that if you don't work your customer base in the first place it is never going to work for you. If you couldn't figure that out without me telling you then you are far too stupid for this or any other book to help you.

If you are one of the few that takes the time to work your customer base but are close to giving up, DON'T DO IT! More often than not the best salespeople give up just before they start to truly get ahead in sales. The thing that I don't understand is that instead of changing careers completely most go right into another sales job or another company doing the exact same thing. Those that do this are the same ones that have to sell until they die.

A DIFFERENT LOOK

I have always stressed the importance of maintaining your relationships with your customers. If you don't maintain those relationships then you are going to have to work much harder. You will have to develop new leads just like the new salespeople rather than allowing those that you have already sold to do the work for you. It is for this reason that I have always been much more successful using a social close as opposed to a much more direct aggressive close.

One thing that I have always noticed in my own personal experience is that the more gentle approach was always much more effective long term than beating my customers into signing a contract. Sure you may get more sales by beating your customer into submission but what are you giving up?

With every customer that you speak to you have to consider how your approach is ultimately going to impact not only the initial sale but your long term relationship with that customer. If you push too hard you may get that initial sale from that customer but they aren't going to refer their grandmother to you out of fear that you are going to stop her heart with your sales onslaught. Sure you want to get the sale but you have to be aggressive while still being considerate and tactful.

A good way to look at each customer is to consider them to be someone that you know but not too well. A good example of this would be a cousin that you see on a semi-regular basis. You aren't going to beat them into signing up for whatever it is you are selling, you are going to help them make a decision, and then proceed with the sale.

A true salespeople can be convincing without be forceful. A true salespeople can develop relationships with every customer that extend beyond the final signature. I could hold a gun up to every customer and get them to sign the contract but it takes talent to get them to sign because you have persuaded them to your way of thinking.

If you are able to walk away from a sale without thinking about whether they are going to back out or not you SOLD IT. If you walk out of the sale wondering whether or not they are going to cancel then you probably held a gun to their head. Sales should never be comparable to a hostage situation. If it is I assure you your customer isn't going to leave the sale feeling comfortable nor are they going to talk about you positively to friends and family.

Every sale that you attempt needs to be looked at as a stepping point towards future sales. If you can't build a positive situation for the customer from the beginning then they are going to feel as comfortable with referring you in the future. Your goal with each and every sale should be to create a memorable and purely positive presentation that leaves you and your customer feeling good about everything that happened. Any regret they have could mean lost sales for you down the road.

You have to remember that each person is connected to someone else. That someone else is connected to other people. Those other people are connected to even more people. I could go on forever with this until every person in the world is in some way to connected to each other through a massive social network. Your goal is to look at the bigger picture and attempt to tap into as much of this social network as possible and let their voice speak volumes for you. Many can be heard much louder than the few. The more you build your network the louder your voice will be.

A good way to think about it would be to picture it as if it were a tree. While you could just focus on the trunk itself there are numerous branches with smaller shoots and leaves. Sure the trunk is the obvious place to start but if you start branching out your one small sale could become numerous sales. These numerous sales could turn into even more sales and it just grows from there. It is important that you take full advantage of this. It is one thing to understand the concept, it is another to act on it and take full advantage of these social networks that are available to you.

Knowing how hard you need to close each customer to be effective can be the most difficult part of every sale. If you close too hard you risk losing the opportunity for referrals. If you don't close hard enough you risk losing the sale completely. It is truly an art determining what you need to do in each individual situation and one that you will slowly master with time. I wish I had the perfect formula for it, but I really don't. This is something that you must learn on your own with experience. I assure you that surgeons don't know what to do in every situation when they have the body opened up and ready to operate. They are going to lose a few patients before they understand what they need to do in order to save many more. Selling is similar. Success takes time and practice. With this practice will come the added self confidence that a salesperson can never get enough of.

LONG TERM ASS KISSING

It is important that you think of each and every sale as future opportunity. The customer that you sold could need another service from you down the road. They could have a friend that will. They could have a family member that will. For most salespeople once a sale ends so does the relationship with the customer. Rarely is thought given as to what could happen long term. While you may not notice much of a different short term by keeping these relationships it is what separates the elite from the bottom tier long term. Work hard now to obtain success for yourself into the future.

Think about it this way: every referral that you get is a gift. The odds of you closing that sale are huge. You simply can't get much closer to having a sale given to you than to receive a referral especially from a family member.

Assuming that you close out every referral that you get (and you probably should) and it you sell 1 out of every 10 sales calls you would require ten fewer leads for each referral you receive in a month to generate the same income. So if you were to generate 5 referrals per month you would require 50 fewer leads per month to make the same income. This of course can make a major difference in the amount of effort you have to apply to marketing yourself as well. So while your family might have a hard time with how hard you work in the beginning that hard work will pay off large dividends down the road. However, this increase in referrals does have disadvantages to it.

The problem with seasoned salespeople with a strong referral base is that rather than continually producing the same number of leads on a monthly basis regardless of the number of referrals that they receive, they become complacent. This becomes an issue because sure they may make the same amount of money while working less, they are giving up a considerable amount of potential new income. As you run fewer leads you are going to reduce the number of new referrers that are available to you and potentially you could slow your lead flow down completely.

By working hard throughout your career and taking full advantage of each and every opportunity you are going to continually grow your income rather than see it stagnate. You are going to see your lead flow from referrals continue to grow until you reach a point where you don't have to do anything but referrals. If you make it to this point then you know that you have run the program properly and you know that you are making as much as you possibly can with the talent that you have created over the years.

Unfortunately, you probably aren't that good yet. You haven't been doing this for years. You still aren't closing like a professional and you have to work your ass off. So rather than thinking about what "can be", bring yourself back to the reality of here and now. You have nothing. You lead flow sucks. Your referral base could use some help. Fortunately, it is never too late to change how you operate. It is never too late to make a decision to work just a bit harder to give yourself the best opportunity possible long term. You just have to dedicate yourself to the process!

LET IT FLOW

As discussed earlier you are now going to harness the referral power of each and every one of your customers. While this can be done in numerous ways there are some methods that are much more effective than others.

DIRECT APPROACH – While you are talking to the customer you can simply ask for referrals. Some salespeople will ask a customer to write down a couple of names in exchange for a few bucks off their product/service. Some will simply tell them that they are going to call them in a few days to get a list of friends/family. Finally, some just tell the customer that they rely on their referrals and hope that leads come in. While this approach typically has minimal immediate impact it does set a precedent for referrals. It lets the customer know that you benefit from them sending you business and that you appreciate it. If you have a referral program that rewards the customer for referrals this would be an excellent opportunity to mention it to them.

INDIRECT APPROACH – This is the approach that I use more often than any other method. While I always ask for referrals I find that the indirect model is where I get more leads than any other method of obtaining referrals.

With the Indirect Approach you really have to work a lot harder to make it effective. With each and every customer that you sell there should be some type of a file that you create for your own personal records. This file should give you the customer's information, what you sold them, how much they paid, and of course the different methods of contacting them. You should also consider obtaining information such as the day of their anniversary, birthday, or other important dates. This information can prove invaluable to you down the road.

Once you have all of this information about your customers you should arrange the files by date. If you have the customer's birthday then you arrange the files by the date of their birthday. If you do it by anniversary you do the same for that. If you want to keep track of both their birthday and anniversary I suggest making a duplicate copy of the file and placing it each date so that you remember both.

Now that you have yourself setup you should consider sending our birthday cards, anniversary cards, holiday wishes in December, etc.

You could do this by sending an actual card or you could do this through email. The idea is that you are going to give that customer a reminder of who you are and what you did for them. More than anything else you are attempting to keep your name on the tip of their tongue but you have to do so in a way that is somewhat covert if you want them to take notice.

When you send out the card or email you need to include your contact information but make sure that you don't make the message about selling them something. Give them a genuinely warm greeting with your information in the signature of the email or simply on an enclosed business card. You already sold these people so sending them another sales pitch isn't going to help your cause. If they want your service they will remember who you are and give you a call. If they know someone that needs you they will realize it at this time and have them give you a call. This isn't the time for you to go for another close. This is a more passive means of generating the sale.

I have always sent out cards for the holidays and emails for birthday and anniversaries. I found that while this is effective in controlling costs it also meant that I was able to take advantage of multiple forms of media in contacting my customers. By doing this I had more opportunity for my message to reach them. You have to keep in mind that often times customers will change their email address or their physical address. By using multiple forms of communication you are giving yourself the best opportunity to reach them in one way or another.

In my holiday cards I would treat them just like I would my family members and would even include a picture of my own family. By doing this you are going to show them your human side and take them off the defensive. This can be hugely effective in redeveloping trust, especially when you are dealing with families. Sharing who you are with your customer allows them to better understand you and realize that you appreciate their business and that you care about their family. After a few years of this you almost become a member of the family to these customers. They begin to trust you as if you were related and will look to you for anything that they or anyone else that they know needs.

Once you start sending our cards you should realize that you will start receiving them as well. This is especially true the longer that you keep in touch with your customers. As they see you as more of a family member they are going to begin to treat you as such and include you. Once you start receiving these messages you now know that you have a customer for life. These are the customers that you may want to pay extra attention to because they are going to be your best referrers over time.

When you begin receiving cards from your customers it may be a good practice to save those cards. If a customer writes you a letter it is a good idea to save that as well, even if it is a negative one. These cards and letters will not only give you motivation to work harder and become better they can assist you in developing an overall picture of who this family is and what you can do to help them into the future. It will also serve as a reminder when you pull their file for future visits with them.

The greater the loyalty you create with your customers the better chance you have of receiving greater business opportunities from them. These customers probably aren't going to price shop whenever they need to purchase your product/service again and they aren't going to think twice about referring you. If you can get several customers like this then you are going to notice your referrals increasing drastically over time. If you can get several members of the same family or community as your customers you are going to create even stronger bonds where even their children will use you as they grow older without a second thought.

One thing that is VERY important to remember is that the customer contact information that you have should NEVER be abused. I hear all of the time that you should use it to send out monthly newsletters about promotions. While this does work for some people, I find it annoying as a consumer myself. Personally, I have found that simply sending out the messages 2-3 times per year just for the purpose of wishing your customer and their family well is MUCH more effective than regular marketing to them. You want them to remember you in a positive way if you are looking for long term referral success. To me SPAM isn't the best way to generate positive thoughts which is why I have always stuck to special events for communication.

HOME STRETCH

More than anything else, remember that you need a customer base in order to work it. If you don't work hard to generate leads in the first place you aren't going to have anyone to refer you business. This section of the book only matters if you put in the effort to build the business first. There is far more to selling than just convincing a customer to your way of thinking. If you don't put in the time to get the customers and then work equally as hard to keep them you are never going to make it in this career.

Those that work hard and dedicate their day to selling are going to reap the benefits down the road. I don't care if you have to post a picture of a pile of shit on your mirror so that you see it each and every morning you have to find a way to stay motivated. It is tough going through the motions each and every day but those that are able to do it have the ability to make an income that is only capped by their determination. There aren't many jobs that you are able to truly get paid what you are worth. When you are in sales you are getting paid exactly what you are worth. If you don't work hard then the reality that you aren't worth shit is going to hit you hard. If you push yourself, stay dedicated, stay hungry, you are going to boost your value considerably.

Don't let sales shit you out! Work hard now so that sales can take care of you in the future. You don't have to be the best closer, you just have to outwork the best and you can become more successful than anyone. Just like a sport, you have a skill. If you push yourself even when you aren't in front of customers you are going to perform at a much higher level throughout your career. I cannot stress it enough, **DO NOT BECOME A PIECE OF SHIT**!

CHAPTER 9 :
BECOME THE
BADASS

Having read through everything in this book isn't going to make you a better salesperson. The actions that you take after reading this book will. It is truly up to you whether or not you use the information here positively or if you simply ignore it and go back to doing what you were doing before. If you push yourself and truly use what I wrote here in the book you are going to benefit from it.

I know that I am not the best writer in the world. I know that I don't have the best advice in the world. What I do know is that I am realistic. I know that not every method of selling is going to work for each and every person. This is why I focused this book towards the other aspects of selling that can make you successful without simply going over closing techniques.

You can be the shittiest closer in the business and still outsell your counterparts if you outwork them. I have seen great salespeople outsold by lesser ones numerous times. The difference was effort. As you become more successful and gain confidence in your abilities you can't forget what got you there in the first place. Those that allow their success to make them forget what got them there are the ones that have the most difficulty adapting to a tough economy. They don't know how to adapt and go back to working hard to make the sale. If you never abandon that work effort from the start you are going to put yourself in a position that will ensure long term success and stability no matter how poor the economy may be.

The most important thing that I hope you take from this book isn't that you have to be an amazing closer. I hope that you understand that you have to push yourself and learn to work for yourself in order to make it. You have always had the ability to make money in sales you just have to pull it out. Sure the ability to close out 75% of your sales is great but if you have the ability to generate 75% more leads, get 75% more referrals, you are going to generate for more business than that person closing 75% even if you are only closing 25%.

Being a Sales Badass is truly a frame of mind. It doesn't mean that you are supposed to go out there and be a jackass to every customer that you come across. It doesn't mean that you have to be arrogant and cocky. Being a badass means that you are able to push yourself to be the best. You are able to educate yourself. You are able to see the future and push yourself towards accomplishing it.

As a Badass you need to have that confidence that everyone else notices. You need to do the things that nobody else does because you know that is what will make you the most successful. You need to push yourself even when nobody else is. By reading this book you need to take the time to really examine who you are and find a way to become better. Everyone has room for improvement it is just a matter of taking the time to implement those changes.

To make it a little bit easier for you I am going to go back over everything that you need to create your inner badass.

STEP 1 :

Create a schedule for yourself. Those that create schedules for themselves are going to be far more successful at completing their tasks in a timely manner than those that do not. If you intend on sending out mailers 30 minutes per day in the beginning of your shift, then make sure you include that in your schedule. If you want to make phone calls at the end of the day set your schedule to include that as well. By setting the schedule it will push you to achieve those daily goals and will make you much more effective throughout your day, your week, and your career.

An important part of scheduling should also be to create rewards and punishments for achievement or lack thereof. For me this would mean going to Starbucks if I achieved my goals for the day prior or getting to eat at a restaurant. For the days when I didn't achieve my goals I would have to drink office coffee and eat a brown bag lunch. These aren't going to work for everyone but they give you an idea that you can use your own personal desires to help you achieve your goals. I love my luxury foods and beverages and because of that I know that I will push myself harder.

Over time you will train yourself to adapt to the added work ethic. This is the same as if you purposely wake yourself up a few hours earlier so that you can workout every day. Once your body adapts to waking up early this will become a normal part of your daily life. The same is going to be true with adding additional responsibilities to your daily plan.

While adding these responsibilities to your daily plan will make your day a little bit more solid your goal shouldn't be to work longer. There is nothing good about working yourself to death. This will have a negative impact on your health as well as on your person life. The idea is that you work harder during the time that you are scheduled to work. If you want to work 50 hours per week then make sure that you are actually working 50 hours per week. One thing that I hate is hearing that people don't have enough time in their day but when you truly examine their day you realize it is filled with gaps.

Do you really need an hour to take lunch? Can you talk to your coworkers in the morning while filling out envelopes and stuffing them? You don't have to avoid the social aspects of your job just make sure that you are doing productive things while socializing. I have done my fair share of socializing throughout my life but during my set work hours I have attempted to do something productive at the same time. In fact, this is how I started doing mailers so heavily in the first place. Sometimes it just takes that little extra bit of determination to be better than those around you. Don't let the lack of success by others take away your own personal success. Set the example don't let them be the example.

As a family man myself I think part of your schedule needs to include your family. While my coworkers would always make fun of me for scheduling in my family in sales it can be important. Setting a set drop dead time will not only give your family an idea of when they can expect to see you but it will always give you a time to accomplish all of your tasks by. If you hit that time and you don't get it done you don't get extra time to finish it. That is the time for your family. That is the time that you scheduled and it is an appointment that you can't afford to miss.

The reasoning behind being so firm on your appointments with your family is because they are the ones that are going to stand behind you no matter how badly your day goes. You are going to get more motivation from those that love you than you ever will from yourself. Do right by those you love and everything else will fall in place. If you are constantly letting them down your personal life is going to fail and it is impossible to be successful with the world around you falling apart. So make the time. Make it your most important appointment. If you aren't able to make that appointment it is probably because you didn't work hard enough throughout the day. Don't take your lethargy out on your family. Work harder during your work hours and you'll never have to work during your personal hours.

STEP 2 :

Equally as important as scheduling is the creation of personal goals. While this also happens to be the most overlooked aspect of the process it can be incredibly important towards achieving your current and future success.

As part of the goal process you need to determine what is important to you. If you have a physical goal that you are attempting to achieve your goal process can be much easier. This could be a boat, a new car, a new house, or even the ability to pay for an engagement ring or a wedding. By having these types of goals you have something tangible that you are able to strive for. If you have nothing to strive for your goals aren't going to have as big of an impact as they would otherwise. It is also important to realize that a goal that isn't realistic is just as bad as not having a goal in the first place.

Once you have an established goal you need to set a time frame for obtaining this goal. Assume that your goal is to sell $40,000 so that you have the extra money to buy your dream car by the end of the year. Knowing that you goal is $40,000 per month you should now create weekly and daily goals. If there are 4 weeks in a month you know that you have to sell $10,000 per week. If you work 5 days per week in a standard week then you have to sell $2,000 per day to obtain your goal. You now have a means of monitoring the obtainment of your goal on a daily, weekly, and monthly basis.

Remember, this goal should be something that can be obtained. If you make the goal too difficult then you aren't going to achieve it in the first place and are going to beat yourself up for not reaching it. If you set your goal for $40,000 per month but you have never sold more than $15,000 you aren't even going to come close to obtaining your goal. Be more realistic in your goals while still making them a challenge to obtain. By doing so on a regular basis you are going to push yourself to be better and accomplish more than your standard production.

What I always did to monitor my goal is to actually set a chart that starts with $40,000 on day one and shows how much I have to average in sales per day in order to obtain my goal. If my daily average went about my daily goal then I would work on a Saturday in order to make-up the additional sales. To make this easier on the family I would assume that I am working 6 days a week unless I am ahead of pace and then I would take off Saturday and make it a family day. This way the expectation is that Saturday is a workday and if I am doing well the family will get the benefit of it. Everything that I would sell on a Saturday would become a bonus sales day and would assist in catching me up to my goals or putting me further ahead of them.

DO NOT MAKE SATURDAY PART OF YOUR GOAL! Doing this is setting the precedent that you HAVE to work six days a week and will make it far easier to get burnt out in the process. It will also give you reasoning for not working as hard to work during the week. I have heard on numerous occasion salespeople rationalizing their lack of effort during the week by stating that they can simply work on Saturday to make up for it. The psychology of this is absolutely idiotic and results in less positive effort throughout the week.

Once you are able to track your monthly goal with daily averages you could also do the same with your annual goal. By doing this you are going to create a sense of urgency during the end of months when you are blowing your sales goal away. It helps to push you to work harder as a reminder that you have so much more to sell in order to accomplish your ultimate goal at the end of the year.

As you obtain your goals you should always create a new one immediately. Reward yourself for the accomplishment and set a new goal so that you constantly have something to work towards. Just make sure that your rewards are important to you. I can't stress how worthless a goal is if you are aiming towards something that you really could care less about. If you don't like traveling then you probably shouldn't create a goal that involves travel. By creating goals that are meaningless you are setting yourself up for personal sabotage.

A good example of this would be to create a personal goal that involved selling enough to afford to go home for the holidays. If you hate your family, you hate that town, and you hate the holidays this is going to be a goal that you may work hard NOT TO ACHIEVE. By having a goal of this nature there is a great deal of opportunity for you to obtain joy by not hitting your goal because you don't actually want to accomplish it. You may mean well in going home for the holidays but if it isn't something that you actually want that actually means something important to you then you aren't going to work as hard to obtain it.

STEP 3 :

Now that you have goals and you have a schedule it is important to work towards long term growth. Without the ability to grow long term none of the scheduling or goal creation will even matter. Part of creating the long term growth is the establishment of your marketing plan and your referral programs. By creating these programs early on in the planning phases you are going to make your life much easier initially and long term as well. It is important to establish a standard that you are going to go by with each and every sale or attempt at a sale.

MARKETING PLAN

I am sure that nobody will disagree just how important it is to have a marketing plan in sales. If you don't setup your marketing plan effectively then you really can't expect to maintain your sales over time. By creating a solid plan from the beginning you are going to establish a mindset that is marketing first and will hopefully assist you in maintaining a solid marketing plan.

As part of the marketing plan creation you really need to determine what you are going to include in your marketing mix. This could be any number of activities but you should really focus on the ones that you feel you are the best at and that you obtain the best results with. The key is to remember that it is called a marketing mix because you really should have a mix of programs running at the same time for the best results.

Personally I think that mailers should be part of every marketing mix. This isn't because they are the most effective. It is because it is so simple to accomplish. You can do mailers while you are socializing, while watching television with your family, while sitting in front of a house waiting for an appointment, during lunch, etc. A mailing program is such a simple one to do throughout the day it can be used to fill gaps without wasting your overall opportunity to be productive during your set work hours.

Another great program to run as part of your marketing mix is to include door hangers. Just like mailers door hangers give you the ability to fill your day. Rather than sitting around or shopping between appointments or during downtime you should take full advantage by knocking on a couple of doors, hanging fliers, or even by doing some door to door solicitation of businesses. There are a lot of methods of marketing that can be utilized to fill your day and make you that much more productive. By doing these types of marketing during your regular day you aren't going to notice just how much you are doing and by doing it in small pieces daily it isn't going to be quite as boring when you do it either.

As part of your marketing plan you need to establish times that you are going to set aside to marketing alone. If you want to set thirty minutes of your morning for mailers and fifteen minutes for emails to customers then you should add that to your schedule. By adding it to your schedule you are going to be making a commitment to yourself and it will become another part of your daily goals. You have to achieve this goal before you can move on to your other goals and should help to push you harder throughout the day to accomplish everything before you go home to your family.

If you are finding that your marketing mix just isn't working for you then try mixing it up a bit more. If you have extra time throughout the day you could even try adding more marketing to your mix in order to give yourself better results. The more marketing you do the more results you are going to have. The harder you work in the beginning the easier it will be to get your referral program running and assist in making your day to day life that much more relaxed.

REFERRAL PROGRAM

The first part of creating your referral program would be to create an area where you can store your customer files. This can either be an electronic filing system or a paper one just remember that you need to back it up regardless of how you create it. Without a backup you are setting yourself up for a potential catastrophe that could ultimately wipe out your customer base and thus huge potential for future growth.

I have already established in "Milking the Cow" what needs to be done in order to create a successful referral program. This is the part of the book where you actually create it. You need file folders or a database in order to manage your customer base. As you create your leads you should also create a customer folder. As you meet with your customers you should update that folder adding in contracts, adding in personal notes, and of course updating a sheet for each customer that includes important dates such as their anniversary or birthdays.

If you create an electronic database with this information make sure that you create it in a manner that will allow you to easily track these important dates. Reminders can be an important aspect of an electronic program as it could automatically remind you of important dates that are coming up or just happened. This will make your life much easier on a day to day basis in the beginning when you don't have something happening each and every day.

The customers that you don't sell should also have a folder to keep track of them. Just because you didn't sell them initially doesn't mean that you have lost all opportunity to sell them. For this reason you should treat them just like your customer base and send them out the same greeting cards, the same well wishes as you would the customers that you did sell. This should all start with a Thank You card to remind your customer that you exist and that you appreciate them giving you the opportunity to meet up with them. As you send out these types of greetings you should keep track of it so that you know just how much effort you have put into creating more sales and referrals with each customer over time.

GETTING GOING

With all of the basics in place you are ready to go out and sell harder than you ever have before. No matter how much I resisted organization and planning early on in my sales career, I have realized over time that I was just making my life much harder. Once I finally gave in and organized myself and started working harder during my set work hours I realized that I was selling considerably more. I was amazed with just how much free time I had throughout the day even though I thought I was working my ass off.

You are in a career that is going to be both difficult and rewarding at the same time. If you establish your goals from the beginning and create a schedule that can be completed each and every day you are going to be far more successful. More than anything it doesn't come down to being the best closer, it doesn't matter if you are great at using tie downs, and it really doesn't even matter that you know every technical detail about your product/service, effort is what will set you apart and help you to get ahead. If you are willing to work hard in the beginning everything else is going to fall in line. If you see more customers you are going to become better at selling. With more customers you are going to learn more about your products and services and you are going to become more technical.

By scheduling properly you are going to make it easier to see more customers in a day, you are going to be able to do more marketing, and you are going to be able to do all of this without extending your work day. You are already working you might as well put in that extra bit of effort and you will find that you are going to quickly grow not only as a salesperson but as a human being in general. It is amazing at how much that extra work ethic can impact the rest of your life but it truly does. It is up to you to make that happen and make the decision to make a change. If YOU aren't selling right now it is because YOU aren't doing everything that you can.

Take responsibility for yourself and find a way to make yourself better. This is the road to truly becoming a *SALES BADASS*. Embrace it and you will become incredibly effective and will in time become one of the best.

Made in the USA
Lexington, KY
04 January 2011